The Foundations of Divine Union

A Practical Workbook for Inner Union

By **Acacia Lawson**

Copyright © Acacia Lawson, 2025

Layout & Cover design: Mehrab Meraj

All rights reserved. This book or parts thereof may not be reproduced in any form, stored in any retrieval system, or transmitted in any form by any means—electronic, mechanical, photocopy, recording, or otherwise—without prior written permission of the author, except as provided by United States of America copyright law.

For permission requests, write to the author at info@byacacia.com.

The information given in this book should not be treated as a substitute for professional medical advice; always consult a medical practitioner. Any use of the information in this book is at the reader's discretion and risk. The author cannot be held responsible for any loss, claim, or damage arising out of the use, or misuse, of the suggestions made, the failure to take medical advice or for any material on third-party websites, books or movies.

*For my Divine Union Counterpart,
my Person, my Husband, my Best Friend...
Thank you. I love you.
This ride is starting to make sense now ;)*

Contents

Introduction 07
What is Divine Union? 13

Part 1 17

Section I:
Inner Work and Healing 18

Section II:
Clearing Blocks 125

Section III:
Balancing Your Nervous System 185

Part 2 201

Section IV:
Activating Your Soul Purpose and Gifts 202

Section V:
Aligning to your Inner Union 216

Section VI:
Consciously Creating Your Divine Inner Union 229

Section VII:
FAQs and Next Steps 237

Introduction

If you're here, then you're on the journey towards inner Divine Union. You already know that this is not a path for the faint of heart, and there will be many trials and triumphs, ups and downs. All to make way for the clearing out of our cells and bodies for the inner union to take place.

I was blessed to know nothing about Divine Union when I started my spiritual journey. I say blessed because there are so many false teachings out there that we have to discern the truth for ourselves, and I was in no way, shape or form able to discern much of anything except repeated dark nights of the soul over and over again.

The more I went within, the more I cleared. The deeper I went, the more I opened up to the Divine. I never fell into worshiping Gods or Goddesses or even communing with anything other than my higher self, which kept me protected from most of the traps and false light games floating around in the spiritual community. However, my light and my Divine Union codes attracted many 'healers' who tried to steal them from me.

When I came into inner Divine Union in 2020, my Counterpart immediately showed up in my reality, which I now understand is the physical side effect of coming into inner union. Universal Law literally states that this is what happens when you are in energetic alignment to the thing that you desire – it must show up in your reality [*The Law of Correspondence and the Law of Attraction, to name two*].

Stephen is that pure guiding light for me, and our union only expands and deepens as we continue our own inner work and our co-creations in this physical reality with Source.

However, there came a time in my online work that I wanted to seek assistance from others, to collaborate, to find my soul tribe. That was when I had to wise up and stop pretending that I was 'just like everybody else' or that everyone was only wishing 'love and light' on everyone else in the community. People were putting implants on others, using black magic and other nefarious means to steal codes and ideas from other lightbeings, healers, leaders, and that was just the beginning.

After many hard-learned lessons by those I considered friends, clients and guides, I was able to discern.

Thus, I was able to understand more about my own soul coding and power, and how to assist people even more with my work. Specifically, my work is meant for people of my soul lineage, my soul tribe, many whom I have soul contracts with to assist on Lady Gaia at this time; beings who have a similar coding which enables them to reach inner union in this lifetime (if they so wish to do the inner work).

Because not everyone is cut out for this deeper calling and initiation into Divine Union. Many truly want it and seek it out - but few understand the dark depths you must plunge into for the clearings to take place on a dna level. Only with the return of the true organic blueprint codes of the soul can Divine Union be activated internally. This work is all internal work - which then changes your entire external reality. It is not for the faint of heart.

We are the light, and so many of us here are simply to live this by example. But first, we must shine the light on the darkness within ourselves so that we can truly see what is external darkness as well.

When we can see the dark, we can heal, cleanse or remove it from our energy field. So that we can shine brighter and attract more of our soul people, our birthright to live in love, peace and harmony with this planet, and our ever-expanding relationship with Source magnifies even more.

This workbook was birthed out of my own lived experience and embodiment, and also because my higher self and spirit guides said that "it was time" – don't even get me started on my resistance to compiling and writing this workbook. Even though most of this workbook is from information, practical steps, and questions from work with my clients (based on what I did first within myself), there is new information that is streamed from the higher realms as well. It also contains material from my numerous lifetimes as a Priestess – Rose, Druid, and Isis, to name a few.

It is worth noting here that I have done every single exercise in this workbook. I only write what I have done myself; that is my commitment to this path and to the integrity of my own work with my clients and this workbook.

My goal with this workbook is for you to lay the foundations of inner sacred (Divine) union, so that you know no more separation from the Divine (Source). So that internally, you are self-sovereign and stand in your power, no matter what. So that you can have the healthiest, most loving relationships – with yourself and with others – on Gaia, at this time.

I love you. I am proud of you for doing this work. You are guided, protected and loved. Remember to be gentle on yourself as you work through these questions and suggestions. There is no right or wrong way to do this work.

There will be a lot of healing and letting go (tears/anger/grief, old beliefs, etc.) that happens here. So *allow time for integration and rest days*. Don't try to rush through it -> allow it to sink in and really assist your clearing to your original templating. Reread it. Rework it. Know that healing is by layers so you might have to come back to something to heal an even deeper layer.

Because as within, so without.

When you are filled with inner peace, love, balance and the union of your inner masculine and feminine -> that is what you will attract towards you.

IT IS UNIVERSAL LAW.

I send you so much love, encouragement and strength. I know that you are resilient - I mean you bought this workbook so that means you've been through the ringer already! I know that you are here for the highest good of all. I see you.

And I am grateful for you taking this step for yourself, your soul, your soul group and your community here on the Great Mother.

So let's get this party started...

"I am here, I am here, I am here. I am free, I am free, I am free. I am love, I am love, I AM LOVE!"

And so it is.

Many blessings on your journey,

Acacia

p.s. *This foundational workbook for inner union can take anywhere from 6 months to 2 years to complete. It can take longer to integrate all of the healing and embody inner sacred union fully.*

Your Inner Union Timeline depends on how quickly you truly clear and integrate in your energetic and emotional bodies. It also is determined by what you allow or settle for (this can delay the process).

Remember to give yourself plenty of rest, gentle love, clean ph balanced water, and eat lots of fruit and veggies throughout integration from doing the exercises in this book.

For this workbook to truly assist you, a prerequisite of a childhood trauma healing course (*of at least 6 months*) is a minimum requirement.

Without that trauma healing, there is no way to discern between trauma responses and soul responses.

What is Divine Union?

There are two parts of Divine Union that I will go into: the internal (inner) and the external (physical) unions.

Internal Divine Union

The Internal Divine Union must come online before the external union can manifest in your physical reality.

Internal Divine Union is defined in many ways for the different understandings of the various humans (souls) who are here to come into sacred union. This is not a comprehensive definition by any means, but it is for you to understand the meaning.

Internal Divine Union is the sacred merging and balance between the Divine Feminine and Masculine within you. The sacred marriage of your soul with Source (the Divine). The inner union of the God and the Goddess. The balance and harmony of the yin energy and the yang energy. Etc.

When you have been activated (initiated, tested, trial by fire, showing integrity, dedication and respect) into this sacred union, this allows your external Divine Union to come online.

Because as within, so without.

External Divine Union

Your External (Physical) Divine Union appears/shows up in your reality when you have achieved internal union.

On the road to external union, you will be tested with a false counterpart (or two) to see if you will settle, not uphold your truth, and take the easy/comfy/known road.

Your Physical Divine Union Counterpart is the highest aligned partner for your soul in this lifetime. This person is the person who will walk the journey with you, hold you accountable, continue their own growth path as you maintain yours, and be your laugh partner and lover. This Counterpart is the other side to the coin. They carry the same values, truths, integrity, honesty and love as you do. They are here to co-create with you and are also in service to the highest good of all, to the Divine Plan. Their relationship with Source is a reflection of your relationship with Source.

Within the union, there are tests and forces that come at you (as well as in the internal union) because there are now two of you joined under God (Source), a powerful state of BEing.

This makes you a target because of the light you both hold, yet you are also a beacon for others to come back to Source. Divine Unions come together and assist in raising the vibration of this planet, as well as to anchor in the true family unit (which has been attacked for centuries on this planet). They are a driving force in building the new communities on this planet that are in service to the highest good.

The External Divine Union is a direct reflection of your internal union. So if there is still disconnection from God (Source, the Divine), there is no inner or outer union yet. If there is disconnection with your own inner masculine or inner feminine, or there are unhealed core wounds or traumas, or an unintegrated ego, shadows, or no recognition, relationship or play with your inner child… there is no inner union. *Because all of these aspects make you who you are.*

Which then means that no outer union is possible because the internal energetic vibration isn't of true union.

These internal and external areas are what this workbook takes you into. Areas that we will look at, be introspective and go through practices, exercises and healing methods to assist you in clearing what needs to go in order for your internal union to come online.

As a side note (*because I get asked this a lot from people already in a relationship or marriage*):

Being in a relationship when you begin this work can lead to external changes. If the person is your aligned partner, they will grow and expand as you do this work (by doing their own inner work).

If the person is not aligned as you counterpart and are indeed a trauma bond, they will refuse to grow or do their own inner work while you will come to a crossroads of deciding between your own highest alignment and timeline, or choosing a lower one that stagnates your energy, money, soul gifts, etc. and generally leads to some form of dis-ease.

The choice is always yours, between the lower and higher timelines due to the fact that free will exists on this planet for you to exercise at any time. However, an actual physical Divine Union requires that both partners are equal in their energy vibrations of highest frequencies because they anchor in Divine Love on this planet. They both do their inner work and grow together, activating and initiating each other.

Because as within, so without.

With that being said, are you ready to begin?!

Let's start clearing!

Part 1

Section I: Inner Work and Healing

Step 1:
Let's Get Honest

What I notice with most women who I start working with is that they notice things but don't really delve into them. They are aware of people, situations and environments that they are in, but they don't see this as a reflection of their inner self.

They mentally know the concepts of what it takes to be in Divine Union, but they don't embody it. They have not taken that information from the mental state and lived and breathed it with their entire being.

In order to thrive in our highest timeline (which is what Divine Union is all about), we must really understand what we allow. What we agree to. What we don't say 'No' to. What we show the universe that we will accept more of because we don't stand in our truth or our power -> so the universe keeps presenting us with more of the same.

Everyone has been in this position. Everyone has to learn to walk the path themselves. Nobody can do it for you.

And that's what this first group of exercises is about.

You get to go through every area of your life and see what you are allowing. How honest can you get in this section? How much are you willing to face in order to grow?

Section 1:

When we start aligning with our soul, we can truly be ready to thrive and expand. We take the actions we need to take to get into alignment with our highest timeline. Instead of putting up with things or just allowing, instead of making excuses for ourselves or others. When we take the actions, we build up our own knowing and our strength in our ability to trust ourselves, our own inner guidance (aka: intuition, higher self, heart).

So here we go! Into the journey of getting truthful with ourselves about where we're at right now -> in order to step back and see what we need to do, and where we desire to actually be in this lifetime.

Honesty Exercises

Be honest with yourself in these questions. Only you can reveal what needs looked at by being truthful with yourself.

These questions are good to do more than once, so come back again 2-3 months after the first time you have completed them.

Relationships:

1. Unhealthy relationships - where do you allow people to use you (i.e. to not pay for your services in business, not paying you overtime, or to have sex with you for no relationship/no commitment to true union), take from you (i.e. your time, emotions, money, power), belittle you, take advantage of your kindness/compassion, or use guilt/shame/manipulation to control you or a specific outcome in a situation?

List the most significant relationships or those you have frequent contact with and an example of their behavior.

Relationship/Person	Allowed Behavior

2. Who holds you back, discourages you, gives backhanded compliments, or tries to keep you on their level (family, exes, coworkers, old friends)?

_____

_____

_____

3. The majority of people around the globe grew up in dysfunctional families (i.e. workaholics, alcoholics, martyrs, religious zealots, mental or physical abuse, narcissists, codependents, etc.).

What role did you take in childhood that you are still playing now (i.e. the savior/rescuer, the jokester, the black sheep, the peacekeeper, the nurturer/mother, the fixer, etc.)? Give an example of how you are currently in this role.

_____

Section I:

_____

_____

4. How have you given your power away to your family (i.e. judging, advice giving, making you feel like a child, etc.)?

_____

_____

_____

5. How is your relationship with your mother (or the feminine figure who raised you)? Do you hold any fears, hurt, anger, sadness towards her or how she shows up in your life?

_____

_____

_____

6. How is your relationship with your father (or the masculine figure who raised you)? Do you hold any fears, hurt, anger, sadness towards him or how he shows up in your life?

_____

_____

_____

7. How is your relationship with your friends? Do you have many people you trust and can count on? Or do you feel people easily betray, abandon, neglect or misjudge you?

_____

_____

_____

8. How do you feel about being in a serious relationship/ marriage (i.e. I feel alone, I do everything, I don't trust my partner, I want to leave constantly, I don't trust men/women, Nobody can stay with me long-term, I'm too emotional, etc.)?

_____

_____

_____

9. How are your work/business relationships? Do you give more than you receive? Do you enjoy the people you work with or do you prefer to work alone?

_____

_____

_____

10. What do these answers above say about your boundaries? Would you say that you have good or bad boundaries? (*Any*

Section 1:

boundaries in your personal life will be reflected in your business life and in your health/body. We need to firm these boundaries up in order for you to be successful and live your authentic soul life.)

_____

_____

_____

Health:

1. What is your body saying to you? Are you happy with your physical health? Can you hear your body and what it needs?

_____

_____

_____

2. Are you taking more time for your body and loving it/telling it why you love it and are grateful for it?

    a. How often do you love on your body?

    _____

    _____

    _____

b. Can you look in the mirror, into your own eyes, and tell yourself how much you love yourself and are grateful for your body every single day?

_____

_____

_____

3. How is your mental health? Do you feel anxiety, overwhelm, depression or stress once a week or once a month...?

_____

_____

_____

4. When do you notice any flair ups with anxiety, sadness, anger or other emotions - around certain coworkers, family, strangers, times of the month or year, etc.?

_____

_____

_____

5. Do you meditate? How often? Are you ready to connect with your highest self or do you connect with your higher self every day?

_____

Section 1:

_____

_____

6. When you are stressed, what are the common ways you relieve your stress? Where in your body do you carry your stress?

_____

_____

_____

7. How emotional are you?

   a. Do you express your emotions or stuff them?

   _____

   _____

   _____

   b. Can you identify different emotions you feel?

   _____

   _____

   _____

c. Do you need time to process how you feel or are you able to say in the moment how something makes you feel?

_____

_____

_____

8. Do you express your emotions in all areas of your life (relationships, job, etc.)? Give examples.

_____

_____

_____

9. Do you listen to your intuition? Do you know when it speaks to you and tells you that you need a day off, to take a walk, or to go frolic in nature?

_____

_____

_____

10. What form of exercise do you practice? How often do you practice it and is it in your calendar (structure)?

_____

Section I:

_____

_____

11. How do you give away your power regarding your health (i.e. eating bad food or binge eating, not exercising or exercising correctly for your personality type, holding onto emotions, etc.)?

_____

_____

_____

Money/Business:

1. How is your relationship with money (i.e. spreadsheets, spend and don't look at bank statements, strict budgets, living paycheck to paycheck, etc.)?

_____

_____

_____

2. Do you have joy or anxiety when looking at your money and budgeting?

_____

3. Do you feel you should be making more money?

4. What kind of work would you do if you could do anything or own any type of business?

5. Do you borrow money from your parents, partner, friends or siblings or do they borrow money from you?

6. Do you believe you are controlled by money? Why or why not?

Section 1:

7. How do you give away your power in business?

8. What was your dream job(s) when you were a child or teenager?

9. How are your boundaries around money and business? Do you have firm boundaries or do you let people take from you constantly?

Extra - Creativity:

1. What are 2 things you are really good at (or love to do) that you don't tell people/friends/ family about? Why don't you tell them?

   _____

   _____

   _____

2. What do you do when nobody is watching - dance, sing, tell jokes, read weird books, etc.? How often each week do you do this?

   _____

   _____

   _____

3. What is your favorite hobby? How often do you do it and do you schedule time in your calendar for this?

   _____

   _____

   _____

Section 1:

4. Where do you want to be in 2-3 years? Do you dream about your future or envision it?

_____

_____

_____

5. Do you share similar life goals/desires as your partner/friends/family? *This is important because we need to be surrounded with people who are supportive, share our dreams, and motivate us.*

_____

_____

_____

6. What kind of partner/love relationship do you truly desire? What does it look like? What are your innermost desires?

_____

_____

Step 2: Healing Childhood Trauma and Wounds

There are various ways to go about this, and you might've seen that one of the pre-requisites to this workbook is: *a trauma healing program*.

If you've done any type of healing work, you know that healing is done in layers. Every trauma or wound we experienced in our childhood is multilayered, which means there are many reasons why it happened and different levels in our systems that the trauma touched that must be cleared in order to come back to our original (Divine) template/blueprint.

Yes, you most likely have done some form of trauma work/healing during your spiritual journey. Yes, you might have answered some of these questions before. Yes, you might even believe that you are done with healing your trauma.

However, please do fill out the answers below to the best of your ability and take time to deeply consider the questions and what is coming up for you now to move out of your body (i.e. cry, purge, kick and scream, write or pound a pillow…).

Section I:

Healing Trauma Exercises

It's important to delve into all areas of trauma. We are going to focus on healing your parental and generational wounds, but we will take a look at everything.

Be honest with yourself in these questions. Only you can reveal what needs looked at by being truthful with yourself.

1. Who was/were your main caregiver(s) growing up?

   a. What did you learn from her or him or them about "women" or being a "mother" that you still carry today (i.e. what preconceived notions do you have about staying in a marriage or leaving it due to your mother, every woman is codependent, must be a helicopter mom, etc.)?

   _____

   _____

   _____

2. What did you learn from your main caregiver(s) about "men" or being a father that you still carry today (i.e. all men are liars, you can't trust them, men just leave you and break your heart, too strict/protective, etc.)?

   _____

   _____

   _____

3. Perfectionism comes from judging ourselves harshly (it is a learned trait that can be unlearned).

    a. What areas do you judge yourself harshly in? (i.e. health, love, money, business, life)

    _____

    _____

    _____

    b. How are you accepting yourself, your body, your actions, every day?

    _____

    _____

    _____

4. Continue to write down any negative thoughts about yourself that you are having. Have an internal dialogue with yourself about them to see where they stem from (usually childhood).

    a. Take time to get to the root (core wound) of why you think these thoughts/where they come from and how you can reprogram your mind (use a separate sheet of paper). *For example, you can ask yourself why you feel that way - what version of you thinks/feels this way (7 year old you, 10 year old you). Where did this begin/what memory wants to come up to be cleared and let go of?*

Section 1:

_____

_____

_____

5. What trauma handed down from generation to generation looks like...

   Think about your family history and family tree. Your parents, your grandparents and their parents. Your aunts and uncles. Your siblings. Your ex(es).

   Try to recall any hushed up stories about family members or any stories you hushed up regarding your own relationships. Use the words below to describe your family.

   You might want to use a pencil...

   _____

   _____

   _____

Most family trauma/dysfunction has 2+ behaviors for each family member:

- alcoholic, addict, misuse of alcohol or drugs,
- enabler (of others' bad behaviors or of self),
- religious zealot (extreme or forcing down other's throats/'my religion is the only way'),
- workaholic,

- not following through, heavy debt or big/constant spender,
- neurotic (constant/pathological worry),
- perfectionist (high strung),
- harsh, always critical, verbally abusive,
- dictatorial/militaristic,
- chronically ill or hypochondriac,
- pill popper (prescriptions and over-the-counter),
- "Susie homemaker"/constant caregiver (always thinking of own self/needs last or below everyone else's),
- obese, emotionally ill, hoarder,
- narcissist, sociopath, pathological liar,
- ladies man/player, sexually aggressive, promiscuous,
- violent/glorified fighting, grabbed or wrestled inappropriately,
- thief, inmate/jail sentences, argumentative,
- people pleaser, martyr,
- loner (hyper independent),
- codependent (can never be alone, depends on one person, goes from relationship to relationship, etc.)
- life of the party, pathological charmer

List every behavior from above that your family or adopted family members have:

- **Mom (or caregiver)-**
- **Dad (or caregiver)-**
- **Mom's Dad-**
- **Mom's Mom-**
- **Dad's Dad-**
- **Dad's Mom-**
- **Aunts (mom's side)-**
- **Uncles (mom's side)-**
- **Aunts (dad's side)-**

Section 1:

- **Uncles (dad's side)-**
- **Great-grandparents-**
- **Your Siblings-**
- **You-**
- **Your current relationship partner/spouse-**
- **Your last relationship partner/ex-spouse-**
- **Anyone else you consider family here-**

What patterns do you see in yourself that you can say goodbye to today?

Remember, this is not to blame your family for everything that has happened in your life - but to get a clear picture of any patterns you carry from childhood or from being in a dysfunctional relationship that can still affect your relationships today.

Once we have identified the patterns, we can clear them and see them when they are happening towards us in real time. Then we can detach and start living a very liberated life free of guilt, shame and fear (and health issues, gut issues, etc.) placed on us by our families and society.

1. Who do you feel adds chaos to your life or are toxic (always complaining, always 'shit-talking', always drama around them, etc.)?

_____

_____

_____

2. Have you denied your own needs and taking care of yourself for others' needs and desires (or not to hurt them, etc.)? Do you still do this? If so, how?

_____

_____

_____

3. Do you allow the feelings or possible reactions of others to control you or determine your behavior and choices aka people pleasing (i.e. what would people think if I left my job/partner/town, what would my partner do if I left him/her, I better not do that because I will be seen as bad/nasty/rude, etc.)?

_____

_____

_____

4. How much of your past life/self have you truly let go? This includes letting go of old businesses that are stagnant, old relationships that are one-sided or stagnant, familial expectations or guilt surrounding not keeping the "perfect family" intact or guarding the family 'secrets'.

Ties to old energy will keep you pulled back into the past and the same problems/patterns will arise in your new life if you have not dealt with and/or cut off energy around the old.

Section I:

_____

_____

_____

5. **Do you understand and accept that you no longer have to accept dysfunction, manipulation or toxic people in your life? That you have power over your journey in this lifetime? That you create your own reality?** <u>That you do not have to please others over yourself and your needs</u>?

   This is not just about knowing this deeply, but also about enforcing your boundaries regardless of others' reactions to your boundaries or fear of hurting feelings. We need to make sure there is no need for approval that you are seeking.

_____

_____

_____

Sometimes, sexual trauma occurred in childhood in the home, at school, in childcare situations, etc. If you have experienced any sexual trauma in your life, *please seek an experienced sexual trauma healer or therapist* to assist you in moving that out of your body.

Healing Trauma Tools

Everyone has a different tool that they resonate with that helps them to heal trauma and move the energy out of their body.

I list a few below because these are the modalities that I use and recommend for my clients. *There are other tools that can be used but these are the ones that I find the most helpful.*

It might take a few sessions of this work to start to move the stuck energy. You might have to try a few different ones and on various days, the ones you used before might now work. Be flexible, non-judgmental, and keep at it. You will allow whatever needs to go to be set free, even if it takes a bit of trying!

- Breathwork (*start with grief or anger sessions*)

- EMDR

- Inner Child Dialogue (*more on this in the next step*)

- Energy Healing (*more on this later*)

- Somatic Experiencing

Please seek a qualified coach or therapist to assist you through healing trauma. It is very important that you don't feel alone when you continue to heal trauma and clear those timelines so that you don't loop back into the trauma (PTSD).

The Insight Timer app is also a useful tool for meditations and other modalities to assist in clearing trauma. Find what resonates

Section 1:

for you and your needs, and keep at it. Trauma is layers so don't be discouraged if a deeper layer to the same event reveals itself later on - it is your soul's journey to clear even more so that you don't repeat this in your next life!

Books to read for more information:

The Body Keeps the Score by Bessel van der Kolk,

Healing Your Authentic Self by Alice A. Bailey

Adult Children of Emotionally Immature Parents: How to Heal from Distant, Rejecting, or Self-Involved Parents by Lindsay Gibson

Book, Workbook and Group Support:

Adult Children of Alcoholics and Dysfunctional Families ACA big red book, 12 steps of adult children workbook, online and in-person meetings for support - https://adultchildren.org/

CODA - Codependents Anonymous

Exercise:

Write out a letter expressing a hurt or resentment you carry towards a parent, sibling, past partner, current partner, friend or coworker, etc.

Feel free to write a letter to anyone who you feel anything (fear, anger, sadness…) towards due to their past actions.

As you write, allow yourself to feel where on or in your body the pain sits. Let your body guide you to how it wants to clear these emotions from your pain body (i.e. screaming, crying, raging, punching a pillow, laying on the floor kicking, wailing and sobbing, etc.).

Add anything else to the letter that comes up during you releasing the pain/stuck energy from your body.

Then burn the letter to fully clear those energies.

Do this exercise as many times as you need as the layers of trauma can reveal more that needs to heal or be cleared.

Trauma Loops

Trauma loops are when the trauma hasn't been cleared. This looks like extreme anxiety and catastrophizing. The body goes back to feeling like a scared child again, and goes into default survival mechanisms such as people pleasing, fight/flight, freeze, fawning, etc.

If you notice that you are repeating a pattern or having a trauma response to someone or a situation, try to take a step back and see what the root cause of this reaction is.

- Where does it truly stem from; what is the root wound, lifetime or memory?

_____

_____

Section I:

- What childhood (or past life) event needs to be examined and cleared?

- What soul lesson needs to be learned or integrated here?

- What do I need to do to fully clear this reaction/trigger from happening again in the future (ask your higher self/heart)?

Step 3: Reconnecting with Your Inner Aspects

Firstly, reconnecting with your positive inner aspects is a journey. Not everyone achieves this at the same pace. Some days, you are really connected; other days, there is more to clear/learn/integrate and the connection seems to have disappeared. This is the same for the connection with Source as we continue to clear false programs/traumas/etc. out of our DNA and come fully into our power and sovereignty.

Secondly, each of us has many different inner aspects. It is good to start identifying them and understanding their motivations and how they speak to you. Some are positive influences and some are negative – and we will dive further into this during this section.

I will start with the inner critic.

Inner Critic

This is typically the voice of your mother or father or primary caregiver. It can also be a really strict teacher or another adult who had power over you as a child.

Section I:

The inner critic tells you that you aren't good enough, that you will never do this or that, that you are a letdown/failure, that you're an imposter or a faker...etc.

This voice is harsh, angry, or mean, and is meant to hold you down and not let you achieve true inner union or come fully into your own knowing. It wants you to listen to it and think it speaks truth, but it's a fear based voice that has been passed down to you by someone who lived in fear.

The inner critic likes to kick you when you're down (when you've had a bad day, when something didn't go right, when you haven't slept well, are tired, or don't feel at 100%). This is why it's important to do what you can to keep yourself as healthy as possible, rest when your body says to, and to also know the inner critic's voice.

1. Who does your inner critic sound like?

2. Can you see how this voice has tried to stop you throughout your life?

3. Are you ready to say enough is enough?

"I refute this false programming of the inner critic and I choose to live in my truth and in unconditional love for myself."

Ego

When I refer to the ego here, it is the inner part of you which was created during your childhood to protect you from harm. Some people refer to it as the false self, lower self, negative mind, or their old identity. It started out as a good thing to protect you from trauma in your childhood and it keeps you in survival mode as an adult. *We will discuss the ego more in the next section.*

For now, it is important to understand the ego's voice. The ego likes to convince you to stay safe, to play it safe, and to not do anything out of the ordinary; to stay invisible and not draw attention to yourself; to stay small; to focus on other people's problems/dramas in order to draw attention away from your own needs or healing.

So anytime you try to expand or grow or learn a new way of doing things (especially if that new thing brings up fear in your body or mind), your ego will tell you it's okay if you don't do it. Or it will convince you of why you shouldn't do it - of all the bad things that 'might' happen. How you could 'die' if you choose to go against the grain (of society, your family, your job...).

That was the ego's job (to save you) during your childhood because we grew up in dysfunction, toxicity, trauma.

However, we don't need the ego as an adult - one who takes full responsibility for their own thoughts, actions, and energy.

Look back at a few instances when you were going to change your job or relationship, move to a new location, travel somewhere new or try something exciting. Or even something such as writing your own book or creating a new art piece or starting a new business.

1. What did your ego say about doing that new thing?

2. Did you do it despite the negative voice/opinions coming from your ego?

3. Or did you procrastinate, delay, not do it, or give it up entirely?

Section I:

> *"I thank the ego for its protection as a child but I don't need this survival mechanism anymore. I no longer consent to my ego controlling me. I am aware of its voice and why it pops up."*

Inner Child

Your inner child is beautiful, inquisitive, and usually, your most neglected part. She was made to feel small, silenced and neglected growing up in your childhood home(s). She felt she had no power. That she couldn't say or do what she wanted to do - which was to have fun, to laugh and play, to be free! Or she had to perform in a certain way to get her needs met or to feel safe.

Due to this, she spent a lot of time alone, feeling scared, upset or angry that nobody listened to her true feelings, her very human needs, or her fears. She can cause a lot of chaos energetically (which can show up as people who hurt you, who betray you, hard lessons, illnesses, etc.) until she gets your attention.

It is our job now to reassure her that she is okay, that no matter what we do, we will always protect her and look out for her. That she is always loved and hugged and given space to have fun.

1. What is your inner child saying to you?

2. Have you spoken with her today?

3. Does she need a hug or reassurance?

4. Does she feel your love?

5. Are you making time for her?

"Dear Inner Child, I see you. I am sorry I haven't paid attention to you but I'm here now. What do you need today? I love you. I'm so proud of you!"

Inner Feminine

Oh, the inner feminine! She is that soft, loving voice inside of you.

Some say she is your intuition; that part that wants you to be in the flow (instead of planning every second of your day out, from needing control/ego). She guides you to what your heart truly desires.

If you listen to her, she wants to create with you and assist you in living your fullest life from a heart centered way. She is full of ideas, love and beauty. She looks at the world and sees amazing, wonderful life. She has compassion, grace and unconditional love. Her nurturing presence feels like home.

She will say things to you like: you are awesome, create a specific artwork or story, take more time to rest, eat a specific food, reconnect with nature or put your hands in the soil, go hug a tree or cry next to it, etc.

1. Can you hear her speak to you?

2. What is she telling you to do today for yourself?

3. What does she sound like?

The more we listen to her and ask her guidance, the more we hear her speak to us. Because we were taught to not listen to her during childhood (and whatever else was learned about women based on the society you grew up in), it can take a bit to build up this relationship.

She must feel safe to express to you freely; that you won't judge her or shut her down. That you will respect, cherish and love her.

Inner Masculine

Our inner masculine is another neglected piece. Most of us were taught to be in our masculine at a young age - whether it be through sports, academics, home life or a job. But it was the unhealthy masculine we were taught to be in - aggressive or passive aggressive, obsessed with work, health or 'love', overly systematic or scheduled/planned everything, fearful of criticism or sticking out (as odd, not a part of the pack), etc.

Yet our true inner masculine is very healthy.

He is the action taker who takes his direction from your inner feminine (her ideas or desires). When she is clear on what she sees/desires, she then has direction, and he can take action to make her ideas/goals/desires happen. He aligns everything so that when he tells you to take the specific action at a certain time, it all falls into place easily. Opportunities abound! He has provided for his feminine once again! He is loved and respected for his actions and help. He is given gratitude for his work.

His voice is gentle yet firm. He does not want you to fail or be misguided. He wants to assist you to your highest timeline and <u>he knows the quickest route there</u>. He loves and adores you.

1. Can you hear his voice?

2. What does he say to you?

3. Are you following his leadership/his actions he has asked you to take?

For so many years, we have disregarded our inner masculine's words, his help. This relationship, as with your inner feminine, takes time and dedication to build up again.

Higher Self

Your higher self aspect is a version of you that exists in the 'spirit realm' or the 'higher realms'. Sometimes, this aspect shows up as an older (or younger) version of how you are in this lifetime. Other times, she or he can look like a different species: Fairy, Elvin, Dragon, Lyran, Angelic, Pleiadian, Arcturian, Sirian, etc.

Your higher self can change depending on the day and what you need to know in that moment.

The higher self aspect is able to see the larger picture at all times. They are connected directly to Source, so they are more aware of all the underlying and interconnected energies working in any given situation throughout the universe.

In order to connect with your higher self, I recommend that you start daily while in your meditation practice. Feel/see/sense/hear your higher self come to you in your protected universal space. Ask them to show up in whatever form they wish to take today. When you are ready to see, you will be shown. It's good to have a higher self

Section I:

journal for the questions you want to ask them and to write down their answers (so you don't forget after the meditation is over).

Your higher self will give you guidance on all areas of your life in accordance to the highest good of all. Most people have blocks with connecting to their higher selves, and it takes time to trust in our own senses and third eye in order to see/hear/feel our higher selves.

1. Are you in communication with your higher self every day?

2. Do you feel peace and love from that inner connection?

3. How can you communicate better with your higher self every day?

Meditating daily with your higher self and asking your higher self to reveal any blocks you have to inner union will assist your journey as well. Write down any insights that arise or anything that you need to journal about further. Ask your higher self to assist you or show you any blocks, lifetimes, cords, old beliefs, and patterns that must be cleared from you to step into Inner Divine Union.

Daily Practice:

Each day, practice connecting with your inner child, your inner feminine, your inner masculine and your higher self.

Remember, this is like exercising a muscle. It can take a steady practice of listening for a week or more before answers start to come to you easier. Don't be hard on yourself. Allow the process to unfold. No judgments.

Sample questions to ask:

- How is my <u>inner child</u> feeling today? Does she need a hug or is there anything she needs today? What kind of fun does she want to have today?

    - Write a letter to your inner child, expressing love, compassion and acknowledging any wounds or needs your inner child has in that moment.

    _____

    _____

    - The more you develop this relationship with your inner child, you can start to give her tasks to help you with (creativity or fun for yourself, etc.).

    _____

    _____

Section I:

- Sitting down in stillness and silence, ask your <u>inner feminine</u> to help you with something you desire. Ask her what she would do or how she would act in this situation.

  ▶ How can you hear her better?

  _____

  _____

  ▶ What else does she want you to know today?

  _____

  _____

  ▶ Is there something she wants to create that is a part of your highest timeline today?

  _____

  _____

  ▶ What will bring her more joy and allow her to receive more?

  _____

  _____

  ▶ Write down her answers to refer back to (*so you don't second guess her*).

  _____

  _____

- Once you have clarity for the idea, creation, situation, relationship, etc. from your inner feminine, now it's time to speak to your <u>inner masculine</u>. Ask your inner masculine what step you should take today to achieve this goal/idea (from your inner feminine).

    ▸ What do you need to do today for highest alignment?

    _____

    _____

    ▸ How can you assist him or listen to him more?

    _____

    _____

    ▸ Is there anything he wants you to know today?

    _____

    _____

- When a question pops into your head of something you wish to do or a big step you want to take, write the question down in your <u>higher self</u> journal. During your meditation time (*undisturbed, sitting or lying still, maybe a blindfold on and/or ear plugs in to cut out all noise and light...*), ask your higher self this question you have.

Section I:

- Hear, feel, see, or sense her response. *Write down the response so that you don't forget it.*

　_____

　_____

- Ask anything else you wish to know or learn. If you receive an answer, this is good. If you don't, sometimes you are not ready for the answer or the question isn't relevant to your highest good/timeline (or is an ego/fear based question).

　_____

　_____

- For more assistance with connecting to your higher self, use my meditation <u>here</u>. (QR code for print edition?)

　_____

　_____

After speaking with both your higher self aspect and your inner child aspect, tell them that you love them and are very grateful for their help and love in return. Tell them anything else you wish to say to them. Build up that relationship by communicating with them.

The stronger these relationships are within you, the more you will start to integrate these aspects into your current being. <u>The more they are integrated, the more you will see your outer relationships evolve for the highest good</u>.

Step 4:
The Divine

Our relationship with the Divine is hugely helpful and has, at some point during our many lifetimes, been severed or fractured. In this lifetime, it typically happened during childhood, especially if we were raised with religious parents or around any religious zealotry.

This has led to a less than healthy relationship with our true home and the place we return to -> Source. Energy is neither created nor destroyed and eventually, we understand that we are not separate from Source; we are actually a part of Source.

Some people say that we are all one and that when something happens across the universe, it is felt by all. And, truly, this is the way we remember once we have cleared all of the separation, wounding, and pain we have generated on this karmic and cosmic journey of soul development across many lifetimes, planets, realms, dimensions…

Yet we must begin somewhere and really develop this relationship.

There are many ways to do this work, but I will focus upon Source instead of the Divine Father and the Divine Mother, as both are held within the ALL, which is Source.

Section I:

Generally, people feel better praying to one or the other. Because religion has used the Father to beat into us that women have no or minimal place in religion, sometimes it is easier to picture or feel the Divine as the Divine Mother or the Divine Father.

To begin with, this is okay. Whatever suits you best right now is not wrong. And it can change day by day – some days you will pray to the Divine Mother and other days to the Divine Father. You might feel more inclined to pray to the Mother when you need help creating or healing something, just as you might pray to the Father when you need protection or assistance with an issue.

There is no wrong way here. The only thing that matters is that you are building up a relationship with a higher power that speaks to you. This can be using the name Creator, Universe, God, or whatever works for you.

I have found that eventually on this path, after the Divine Mother and Divine Father parts have been fully healed and integrated within the person, they begin to pray or commune with Source, or God Source, as their higher power. Usually this takes some years to feel this true aligned feeling of the ALL within and without in order to FEEL Source.

It's important to note here that many galactic teams, higher selves, guides, and spirit teams will refer to Source - not God or by any other names.

Higher Power/Source Relationship Exercise

1. How often do you pray or ask for something from your higher power?

2. How often do you express your gratitude to Source (*small and large things*)?

3. How are you building a relationship with Source - *day to day communication, talking, sending and receiving love, asking for help, etc.?*

4. Imagine that Source is pure, unconditional love and only wants you to be happy, healthy and living your highest aligned/best life. What is Source saying to you or trying to communicate to you about your current situation?

Continue to build this relationship up. Try to speak with your higher power every day, even if it's just a quick hello.

It's similar to building a relationship with anyone - communication is key :)

The more you can strengthen this relationship, the more you come into Divine Love, for yourself and for others and all living beings.

The more you feel this Divine Love, the more you step into your soul purpose and service to the Divine Plan, which is service to the highest good of all.

The more that you surrender to the Divine Plan and take the divinely guided action steps asked of you, the more you will come into full

Section 1:

soul embodiment and self-sovereignty -> because this is a part of why you agreed to come here, to fulfill your soul purpose aka your soul mission(s).

Step 5: Shadow Work and Ego Integration

The most common delays and blocks to Inner Divine Union are that the ego and shadow work has not been continuously upheld, or that the ego and shadows have not been truly integrated.

I see this in women who come to me asking why their person has not shown up yet. They have done 'all of the work' and they are in communication with their inner feminine and masculine daily. They only take intuitive actions all the time, every single day.

And that is ego.

Convinced that you have done 'all the work' and there's nothing else to do or look at or clear - that's where the ego gets to be sneaky and convince you that you have done everything you need to do. You can simply 'rest' now. It uses every bit of information you learn (in your head) to talk you out of doing aligned actions that will take you to the next level.

When we get triggered by someone or something, it is because the ego is showing us something. It's not to look at the ego like it's bad. It's to look at it as a helper to show us where we need to look at something even deeper. This trigger will lead us back to a specific childhood or past life event (and eventually to the core wound life) where we were put in this same situation, where a boundary was crossed, where we felt 'powerless'. So the current event itself is simply to show you a wound that needs looked to be at.

Shadows, generally speaking, run around without our conscious knowing. *Our shadows attract other shadows.* So if you are continually attracting a certain type of man or woman in your life, certain events or situations, the most likely culprit is a shadow that has not been seen, healed, and integrated. Many of these can be from past lives.

I will go into what shadows sound or look like later in this section, but for more info on shadows, please see Carl Jung's work.

Ego Exercises:

1. Evaluate how you are bringing negative energy towards you in all areas of your life - work, home, friends, etc.

    _____

    _____

    _____

Energetically, you cannot allow other people's bad experiences, fears and negative views to hold your growth back. If you bring in that energy, that is the energy your new (future) life will have. Be in your power. No more what if's.

You are creating this. Nobody else is.

2. Who am I letting speak into my ear, my life, my soul?

   ▸ Who sways me into not moving/freezing, or moving in the same pattern, or being crippled by fear/avoidance, etc.? (*This is to notice who we are most affected by when they speak to us/give "advice".*)

   _____

   _____

   _____

3. How am I balancing everything in my life right now: work, kids, animals, relationships, partner, free time, creative time?

   a. Do I feel my routine is sustainable?

   _____

   _____

   _____

   b. Where might I need more flow/more time to simply rest, and be on my own schedule?

   _____

   _____

   _____

Section I:

4. How am I allowing the unknown/miracles to happen in my work, my relationships, my life?

   (Are you willing to allow God/Source/Creator to create miracles or are you questioning everything and wearing yourself out by listening to your brain/pain body/ego?)

   _____

   _____

   _____

5. Where in my life do I care too much about what people think of me? My work, my personal life, my health, my persona *(the mask you've created to make a certain amount of money, be 'nice' to everyone, or live the mundane life)*?

   _____

   _____

   _____

6. Do I feel valued? In my life, relationships, and work?

   _____

   _____

   _____

   _____

7. How am I valuing myself?

    a. How does my inner self know I value her/him?

    _____

    _____

    _____

8. What parts of myself do I reject or hide?

    a. Do I feel shame about any part of myself (sexual desires, money, luxury, creativity, etc.)

    _____

    _____

    _____

9. How does my ego protect me, and how does it limit me?

    _____

    _____

    _____

    _____

Section 1:

10. What fears arise when I consider surrendering everything to the Divine every single day?

11. In what ways do I feel disconnected from my true soul essence? My true soul mission/purpose(s)?

12. How can I cultivate more self-love and self-acceptance?

13. What beliefs about myself and the world no longer serve me?

Inner Work and Healing

After many life lessons in teens and early adulthood, everything starts to click and many feel they are most successful after age 40. This goes for many intuitives, soul led people, creatives, etc. <u>This is a quick check to see where you are at right now.</u>

14. Who am I apart from my roles (*daughter, mother, wife, career woman, friend, etc.*) on a soul level? *(i.e. soul mission to help people do..., a galactic guide to..., a love filled food creator, an author of true love codes, etc.)*

_____

_____

_____

15. Does the path you are on currently light your soul up? Do you feel energized and excited by it?

_____

_____

_____

16. Are you on your soul purpose path? Have you claimed your soul purpose fully and completely, committing to doing it no matter what (*this activation can be felt in every one of your chakras*).

_____

_____

Section 1:

17. Where have you been gifted or blessed? (i.e. kindness, business brain, psychic, intuitive, money abundance, New Gaia business codes, etc.)

18. What have you done with that/those gift(s)?

19. Where are you today - stuck, moving forward, flowing, or taking action?

20. What 3 things did you do this past week to have fun?

　_____

　_____

　_____

21. What did you let go of this week?

    a. Did you cry, scream or shake to clear emotions out of your body (instead of keeping them stuck or telling them they are bad/not allowed)?

    _____

    _____

    _____

22. Conduct an ego inventory. Make a list of behaviors, attitudes or desires stemming from your ego rather than your higher self.

　_____

　_____

　_____

　_____

Section 1:

Ego: I froze when my mom called me and yelled at me for no reason. I want someone to rescue me. I feel so alone/I'm always going to be alone...

Higher Self: I have healthy boundaries and did not pick up the call from my mother, I will help myself, I have my spirit team and guides helping me in every moment...

23. List 3 self-limiting beliefs you carry about yourself that no longer serve you. Write why they are untrue. (i.e. *I can't do that which is self-limiting versus I can do whatever I set my mind to which is the soul truth.*)

    _____

    _____

    _____

24. Be mindful of any fears that come up this week and engage them.

    a. Ask why your inner critic/ego feels that way until you get to the root of it -> and then lovingly tell it you understand and thank it for its service but that your soul is in control now and there is nothing to fear).

    _____

    _____

    _____

b. You can also write the fear down if it doesn't go away and then rewrite it how you want it to actually be/turn out for your subconscious practice.

___

___

___

25. Be aware of what you allow every day. **Where do you enable lower vibrational states of others** (i.e. gossiping, unhealthy behaviors, disrespect, feeding addictions, reinforcing their false beliefs, etc.)? *This keeps the false 3D programs functioning due to the ego feeling secure/safe instead of the continued creation of 5D states by upholding healthy boundaries, unconditional love and integrity...*

___

___

___

___

The more you can start to understand your ego and why it does what it does, the more you can start to integrate it every time it is triggered. This is an ongoing process until it is fully integrated (*which can take years*).

Section I:

Shadow Exercises:

These are sample shadows. Some people have more, some have more in the spiritual/energy realms, some have more attached to this lifetime and karma, etc.

Understanding your shadows, bringing them to the light, and either dissolving them completely or integrating them into your current reality allows your true inner light to shine as brightly as the sun.

The reverse of the shadow is the original templating of our souls known as the archetype - the true, heart centered self. I will discuss four main shadows and their archetypes here.

However, there are others which you may or may not already understand, and there are multidimensional shadow aspects (soul fragments) as well. The four shadows and their four archetypes (original soul states) are what I focus on for the foundations of inner union.

1. **Inner/Wounded Child Shadow** [Original Soul Template is the Self-Sovereign Queen]

We all have a wounded Child shadow that sometimes asks:

- "Who am I?"

- "Who is going to do this for me?"

- "Who says I can or can't do this?"

Your values shape your identity. Once you recognize your inherent worth, these values become the dreams of your Child. Do you know your true values? And do you know your true soul desires/dreams?

While the Child dreams, it's the Queen/King Archetype that brings these dreams to life, turning them into physical reality.

It's the difference between "my truth" (Child) and "the truth" (Queen/King, the Sovereign Self).

<u>Signs you might be operating from your Wounded Child Shadow:</u>

- Bending the truth or manipulating situations

- Feeling entitled or overly dependent on others

- Giving your power away repeatedly to others (*parents, spouses, friends, coaches, etc.*)

- Constantly seeking permission or needing constant recognition

- Questioning your identity and comparing yourself to others frequently

- Saying "That's not fair" often

- Being opinionated without considering other perspectives

When in this mindset, you might find yourself:

- Preoccupied with fairness

Section I:

- Expecting life to be easy or protected
- Looking for others' permission to make decisions
- Wanting to dream forever without taking action
- Complaining about situations (creating more problems) without trying to change them (finding solutions)
- Giving up easily and expecting others to fix things

You might hear yourself saying things like:

- "This isn't fair."
- "I'm not allowed to do that."
- "I should check with someone first."
- "I had a dream once…"
- "Who am I really?"
- "What's my purpose in life?"

Reflection questions:

1. Which of these behaviors do you recognize in yourself?

   _____

   _____

Inner Work and Healing

_____

_____

2. In what areas of your life do you allow this Child shadow to take control? (*Consider your relationships, finances, health, career, etc.)*

_____

_____

_____

Remember, acknowledging these patterns is the first step towards embracing your Queen/King (whichever energy feels relevant at the time) - the part of you that knows your power and takes charge of your life.

By recognizing when your Wounded Child shadow is in control, you can start to shift towards your Sovereign Self, making decisions and taking actions that align with your true values and aspirations. This journey from Child to Queen/King is about growing into your own power and creating the life you truly desire.

QUEEN/KING Archetype: the Sovereign Self: the Sovereign Self - Embracing Your Inner Power and Vision

The Queen/King Archetype declares, "This is my vision. This is my dream, no matter what. Every single day."

Section I:

Characteristics of the Queen Archetype:

- Speaks truth boldly and clearly

- Creates life according to their vision

- Uses inspiration to turn dreams into reality and inspires others

- Makes decisions confidently and demands what's needed

- Remains undeterred by others' opinions, approval/disapproval, or actions

- Knows their power without needing to assert importance

When you're in touch with your own Sovereign energy, you'll notice:

- You've achieved a sense of self-mastery

- You take full responsibility for making your dreams come true

- You're less concerned with what's "fair" or "allowed" by societal norms

- You have a clear vision for your life

- You make decisions with ease and confidence

The voice of your Queen says:

- "This is my vision." and "This is who I am."

- "This is the Truth."

- "No one's actions or thoughts have power over my wellbeing, happiness, or sense of self."

- "I am the Source of my own power, happiness and wellbeing."

Reflection Exercises:

1. Envision your Queen life. What would be different about your life if you had created it from a place of total commitment to making your dreams come true?

    ▶ How would your career/business/ creative endeavors look?

    _____

    _____

    ▶ What kind of relationships would you have?

    _____

    _____

    ▶ Where would you live?

    _____

    _____

Section 1:

- How would you spend your time?

  _____

  _____

- What goals would you pursue?

  _____

  _____

2. Observe conversations. Pay attention to the conversations around you, on tv/in movies, or that you're engaged in. Try to categorize them as coming from the Child Shadow or the Queen Archetype.

   Notice:

   - The language used

     _____

   - The level of personal responsibility taken

     _____

   - The focus on fairness vs. vision

     _____

   - The confidence in decision-making

     _____

- The clarity of purpose expressed

  _____

- Are you using the Queen language when you speak or text, or the Child Shadow?

  _____

Stepping into your Queen Archetype is a process. It's about recognizing your inherent power and using it to create the life you truly desire. As you practice this mindset, you may find yourself making more empowered choices, taking bold actions, and inspiring those around you.

Embracing your Sovereign Self doesn't mean disregarding your Child Shadow completely – it means *integrating that child-like wonder and creativity with adult wisdom and power.*

This balance allows you to dream big and then take decisive action to make those dreams a reality.

2. **Prostitute Shadow** [Original Soul Template is the Lover]

We all have a part of ourselves that sometimes doubts our inherent value and that we are Divine (of God Source). This aspect, which is sometimes referred to as the "Prostitute Shadow" often asks:

- "Why am I here?"

- "Why is this happening to me?"

- "Why do others act this way?"

Section 1:

This shadow might make us feel unworthy, but the truth is, we all have inherent values that make us uniquely precious. These values are an integral part of who we are - they're woven into the fabric of our being.

Take a moment to reflect: *Do you know what truly matters to you at your core?*

The Prostitute Shadow tends to act based on what we think we can get from others. In contrast, our Lover Self acts from the heart.

<u>Signs you might be operating from prostitute shadow</u>:

- Compromising your truth, values, desires, or beliefs for others' approval

- Making choices based solely on what you think you can or can't afford (emotionally or financially)

- Struggling with self-worth and fearing/avoiding rejection

- Feeling consumed by the need to belong

- Using your charm/looks/appeal primarily for influence or gain

When in this mindset, you might find yourself:

- Preoccupied with expressing yourself in ways that feel safe and secure

- Constantly bargaining and negotiating

- Saying "I can't afford it" (whether about money, time, or emotional energy)

- Focused more on what you'll get in return than on the process or journey

- Obsessed with pleasing others

You might hear yourself saying things (*out loud or in your head/it doesn't matter because they are there, in your system*) like:

- "I can't afford to…"

- "How much does it cost?"

- "What do I get in return?"

- "What will others think?"

- "I couldn't live with myself if I…"

- "How much will it cost me to not upset anyone?"

- "What's my true passion?" (but not really hearing or listening to the answer)

Reflection Questions:

1. Which of these behaviors do you recognize in yourself?

_____

Section 1:

_____

_____

_____

2. In what areas of your life do you allow this prostitute energy to take control? (*Consider your relationships, finances, health, career, etc.*)

_____

_____

_____

Remember, recognizing these patterns is the first step towards embracing your true Authentic Self (the Lover) - the part of you that knows your true worth and acts from a place of genuine self-love and respect.

LOVER Archetype:

Let's explore the Lover Archetype, your authentic Self – this is all about Embracing Your True Value and Worth.

The Lover Self says, "This is who I am and what I value, no matter what. Period."

Characteristics of your Lover Archetype:

- Lives with 100% integrity to personal values
- Finds safety and security from within, not from others
- Cherishes their own words, opinions, and self-expression
- Communicates clearly and directly, straight from the heart

When you're in touch with Lover energy, you'll notice:

- Your opinions, self-expression, and desires are never up for negotiation
- You're willing to make significant efforts and meaningful sacrifices for what truly matters to you
- Your actions align perfectly with your sense of self-worth (*I will get more into self-worth in another section for the deeper wounds there.*)

The voice of your Lover Archetype might say:

- "This is what I value, and this is what I choose to invest in."
- "I'm willing to make sacrifices for my values, worth, desires, and self-expression."
- "Me, my thoughts, beliefs, and choices are not for sale."
- "I express myself authentically, without seeking anyone's approval."

Section I:

- "My sense of safety and security comes from within, not from others' opinions of me."

Reflection Exercises:

1. Take a life inventory. Look at various aspects of your life (*relationships, wardrobe, diet, clients, possessions, etc.*) and ask yourself, "Do I truly value this?"

    - If it brings you joy, keep it.

      _____

    - If it doesn't, consider letting it go (donation or trash).

      _____

    - Trust your intuition and act swiftly - *there's no need for lengthy analysis.*

      _____

2. Envision your heart's desires. What would your life look like if you were living fully aligned with your heart's true desires, your soul desires?

   _____

   _____

   _____

<u>Write it out in detail.</u> Use an extra sheet of paper.

This exercise can help bring your vision to life:

- Where would you live?

- What work would you do?

- How would you spend your time?

- Who would be in your life?

- How would you feel each day?

Remember, embracing your Lover, your Authentic Self is a journey. Be patient and kind to yourself as you explore and grow. Every step towards living your truth is a step towards a more fulfilling, joyful life.

3. **Victim Shadow** **[Original Soul Template is the Warrior]**

The Victim Shadow often asks:

- "What can I possibly do about this?"

- "What can actually be done?"

The Warrior Archetype, on the flip side, is about decisive action. It's the part of you that turns dreams into reality through practical, actionable steps.

Signs you might be operating from your Victim Shadow:

Section I:

- Constantly bargaining or negotiating

- Feeling overwhelmed by others' emotions

- Being codependent in relationships and blaming others for your circumstances

- Focusing on crises or catastrophes (actual or made up/in the future)

- Feeling a lack of reSources

- Seeing yourself as a burden and dwelling on past failures

- Being bullied or bullying others

When in this mindset, you might find yourself:

- Struggling with boundaries (either not setting them or being too rigid)

- Feeling unsupported or constantly betrayed

- Avoiding risks

- Feeling weak-willed, like a doormat (or treating others like one), and that life is heavy

- Always taking the blame or looking for someone to blame (no responsibility)

- Experiencing or attracting a lot of anger

You might hear yourself saying things like:

- "I don't want to be a burden."

- "Look what might happen." (negatively – never positively)

- "Where's the justice?" or "Why me?"

- "I never get what I want."

- "If I don't do this, everything will fall apart."

- "I have to do it alone." or "I give up."

Reflection Exercises:

1. Boundary check: Where in your life are you not setting up healthy boundaries or asking for support/help to meet your needs?

   _____

   _____

   _____

2. Victim energy audit: In what areas of your life do you allow this victim energy? (*Consider relationships, finances, health, career, etc.*)

   _____

   _____

Section I:

_____

_____

3. Fear exploration: Ask yourself, "What am I really afraid of?" Then keep digging deeper by asking, "Why am I so afraid of that? Will I die or be killed?" until you find the root of the fear.

   ▶ What is at the core of this wound?

   _____

   _____

   ▶ What lifetime is it from?

   _____

   _____

   ▶ Is this fear realistic in your current situation?

   _____

   _____

Recognizing these patterns is the first step towards embracing your Warrior Archetype - the part of you that takes decisive action and creates positive change in your life.

By acknowledging when your Victim Shadow is in control, you can start to shift towards your Warrior Self, making empowered decisions and taking actions that align with your true strength and capabilities. The journey from Victim to Warrior is about reclaiming your power and actively shaping your life, rather than feeling at the mercy of circumstances.

WARRIOR Archetype: The Warrior Self affirms, "This is what I will do/am doing, no matter what. Period."

Characteristics of your Warrior Self:

- Maintains solid boundaries with enforcement
- Shows stubbornness, willfulness, and loyalty
- Demonstrates reSourcefulness
- Experiences abundance
- Willing to take significant risks
- Stays true to their word

When you're in touch with your Warrior Archetype, you'll notice:

- You protect and enforce your boundaries
- You provide unconditional support for your dreams
- You're able to rally support for your cause (energetically and physically)
- You're reSourceful and always find a way
- You take a stand and fight for what matters

Section I:

- You have a high tolerance for risk

The voice of your Warrior Self says:

- "I will do whatever it takes, no matter what."
- "I am the Source of all my reSources."
- "Money comes from me."
- "I'm risking it all."
- "I've got my back/your back."
- "I am not available for that..." (*enforcing healthy boundaries instead of settling*)

Reflection Exercises:

1. Envision operating from your Warrior. How would it feel to always do whatever it takes to make your life reflect your most authentic and fearless self, no matter what?

    ▸ What actions would you take?

    _____

    _____

    _____

Inner Work and Healing

- What boundaries would you set?

  _____
  _____
  _____

- What risks would you be willing to take?

  _____
  _____
  _____

- How would your relationships change?

  _____
  _____
  _____

- How would your career/business/ teachings/creativity evolve?

  _____
  _____
  _____

Section 1:

2. Past and present Warrior: Where have you exhibited the Warrior energy in the past or present?

   ▶ Think about times when you've stood firm in your convictions

   _____
   _____

   ▶ Or recall instances where you've taken risks for what you believe in

   _____
   _____

   ▶ Or remember situations where you've been reSourceful in the face of challenges

   _____
   _____

   ▶ Congratulate yourself on these times! You did that!

   _____
   _____

3. Warrior role models: Do you know anyone in your life who exhibits this Warrior archetype?

- What qualities do they demonstrate?

_____

_____

- How do they handle challenges?

_____

_____

- What can you learn from their approach to life?

_____

_____

Implementing your Warrior is about tapping into your inner strength, determination, and reSourcefulness. It's about standing firm in your convictions and being willing to do what it takes to achieve your goals and protect what matters to you.

This doesn't mean being aggressive or confrontational, but rather being assertive, resilient, and committed to your path. As you cultivate your Warrior energy, you will find yourself becoming more confident, more capable of overcoming obstacles, and more aligned with your true purpose.

Section I:

The process of embodying your Warrior Self is ongoing. Each time that you set a boundary, take a stand for what you believe in, or push through a challenge, you're strengthening this aspect of yourself. Embrace these opportunities for growth and watch as your inner Warrior transforms your life.

4. <u>Saboteur Shadow [Original Soul Template is the Magician] - This is the shadow that engages in self-sabotage, sneakily or overtly.</u>

The Saboteur often asks:

- "When will I see the results?"
- "How will I get the results?"

While both the Saboteur and Magician ask, "How will I make this happen?", the Saboteur comes from a place of anxiety and worry, while the Magician operates from wonder and curiosity.

The Saboteur believes that what's practical and logical is real, while the Magician knows that the invisible (energy) is real.

Signs you might be operating from your Saboteur Shadow:

- Feeling powerless over time (always late, rushing, or bored)
- Making decisions based solely on logic and reason
- Feeling anxious and worried (killing all magic)
- Always procrastinating and overthinking
- Being flaky and unaware

When in this mindset, you might find yourself:

- Giving excuses and reasons why not to do something and avoiding responsibility

- Focusing only on what is, rather than what could be

- Paralyzed by the need to appear responsible

- Needing proof, certainty, and plans before taking action

- Consumed with doubt or feeling clueless

- Lacking inspiration, feeling blocked or bored

- Being rebellious without purpose

- Taking yourself and others too seriously

You might hear yourself saying things like:

- "I don't know."

- "I can't see the way."

- "This is foolish/irresponsible."

- "I need more time. I'll do it later. Someday."

- "I need more evidence, proof, knowledge, understanding, training, certification."

- "I'm blocked." Or "I have no idea."

Section I:

Reflection Exercises:

1. Perfection paralysis: Where are you demanding that everything make sense and be perfectly laid out before you take action?

   _____

   _____

   _____

2. Intuition vs. Sabotage: Do you consider the behavior above following your gut instincts or your intuition? How can you distinguish between the two?

   _____

   _____

   _____

3. Self-Sabotage energy audit: In what areas of your life do you allow this saboteur energy? *(Consider relationships, finances, health, career, etc.)*

   _____

   _____

   _____

4. Challenging "reasonableness": Where are you demanding that your dreams, life, or desires be 'rational' or 'sensible'?

   _____

   _____

   _____

5. Excuse inventory: Where in your life are you making excuses?

   a. What are these excuses protecting you from?

      _____

      _____

      _____

6. Procrastination check: Where are you procrastinating?

   a. What fears or doubts are behind this procrastination?

      _____

      _____

      _____

Identifying these patterns is the first step towards embracing your Magician Archetype - the part of you that sees possibilities, embraces wonder, and believes in the power of the unseen.

Section 1:

By acknowledging when your Saboteur is in control, you can start to shift towards your Magician Self, making decisions from a place of curiosity and possibility rather than fear and doubt. This path from Saboteur to Magician is about trusting in the unseen, believing in your own power to create change, and embracing the magic that exists in every moment.

MAGICIAN Archetype: The Magician Self is the alchemical self, turning lemons into lemonade. Always at the right place at the right time taking the intuitive, aligned action.

Characteristics of your Magician Self:

- Takes energy and turns it into matter (conscious creation/manifestation)
- Activates magnetism & synchronicities
- Unlocks psychic abilities yet is also grounded and graceful
- Not tricked by looking at external conditions

When you're in touch with your Magician, you'll notice:

- You see through illusion and chaos, and are not weighed down by prevailing illusions or beliefs about reality
- You take responsibility for what is, knowing you (your thoughts/beliefs/actions) created it
- You don't need proof, certainty, evidence, plans, or time to act

- You're light-hearted and have a sense of humor

The voice of your Magician Self asserts:

- "I know what I know." And "I am certain."
- "This is what will be."
- "This happens now."
- "I don't care how silly/foolish/irresponsible this looks/feels."
- "I don't have to see how it will all work out."

Reflection Exercises:

1. Envision your Magician life. What will your life look like as you follow your inner guidance and truth at all times?

    ▶ What decisions will you make now?

    _____

    _____

    ▶ What opportunities will you seize?

    _____

    _____

Section I:

- How are your relationships different?

  _____

  _____

- What dreams are you pursuing?

  _____

  _____

2. **Creativity in challenges:** What would your life be like today if, when faced with incredible challenges on the way to getting what you really wanted, you refused to let chaos/ drama distract you and instead decided to get massively creative about overcoming the setback?

    - Think of a specific challenge you've faced. How could you have approached it differently?

      _____

      _____

    - What creative solutions might you have found?

      _____

      _____

    - How would overcoming this challenge have changed your life's trajectory?

3. Energy awareness exercise. Today, pay attention to the conversations that go on - and categorize them as Saboteur Shadow or Magician energy.

   ▶ Notice the language used

   ▶ Observe the energy behind the words

   ▶ How do these conversations make you feel?

   ▶ How could you shift saboteur conversations to magician conversations?

Section I:

Continue to practice this and be aware of your thoughts, actions and words.

Incorporating your Magician Self is about tapping into your inner wisdom, creativity, and power to manifest. It's about seeing beyond the apparent limitations of this reality and trusting in your ability to create change and magic in your life through energy work.

This doesn't mean ignoring reality, but rather seeing the deeper truths and possibilities within it – because we walk in two realities, the spiritual/ energetic realm and the physical realm. SO <u>everything is possible</u>!

As you cultivate your Magician energy, you will find yourself becoming more intuitive, more creative in problem-solving, and more aligned with the flow.

Truly embodying your Magician Self is a process. Each time you trust your inner knowing, take inspired action without needing all the details figured out, or find humor and lightness in a challenging situation, you're strengthening this aspect of yourself. Embrace these opportunities for growth and watch as your inner Magician transforms your perception of reality and your ability to create the life you desire.

Overview Questions:

1. Which archetype do you feel most fits you right now?

   _____

   _____

   _____

2. Which archetype do you want to anchor in more deeply energetically and subconsciously?

   _____

   _____

   _____

3. How can you feel more aligned to all of these archetypes (versus the shadows)?

   _____

   _____

   _____

4. Is there anyone in your life who is close to you who represents these shadows? (*You are who you surround yourself with...*)

   _____

Section 1:

_____

_____

5. Is there anyone in your life who represents all of these archetypes in both words and actions (daily life)? (*You are who you surround yourself with...*)

_____

_____

_____

When we can start to recognize the shadows, and start to respond from our True archetypes, we can start to shift our life in a radical way.

The more you can do this work, the more you will integrate your shadows. *Please use the Insight Timer app for more Shadow Work meditations.*

Step 6:
Past Life Wound Healing

Many women carry pain from past relationships, traumas and cultural conditioning that hold them back from truly loving themselves and others. But what isn't more well known is that all of these issues carry an energetic signature from a 'past life' that continues to loop into this lifetime.

When I refer to past life, it is usually seen in the mind as a lifetime in the past. But time is not linear (like we've been taught), and actually continues in a looping spiral pattern. We came here in this lifetime to transmute all of our karma (in this one lifetime, yay for us!!) from all of our lifetimes that are coexisting right now.

As a soul with many different aspects, we are currently in more than one lifetime at this very moment. With that said, these lifetimes all hold similar (if not the exact same) traumas that we must bring to the surface and then clear.

This is why 'past life' healing is so important. There are many ways to do a past life healing. My favorite is through meditation and higher self assistance.

However, there are other modalities including (but not limited to): past life regression, past life shamanic journeying, Akashic records

Section I:

healings and past life healings. *Please seek a professional for using any of these services as guided by your higher self.*

If you have not done any childhood or adulthood trauma work for this lifetime, I highly recommend doing that work first. If you skip the trauma work and go straight for the past life work, it ungrounds your energy even further from this planet and can create energy leaks, manipulations, hijackings, addiction, etc. It is important to be aware of these situations as they are prevalent in many who choose to skip/bypass necessary trauma work.

If you skip straight into channeling/multidimensional/astral travel work without healing your current life trauma, you are not going to be aware of hijackings or ungroundedness. Your nervous system will be unregulated and your mind/body/spirit connection will be run by ego/child shadows and other beings.

The following past life journey is one that is easy for you to do on your own.

Past Life Meditation

(you can record this as a voice memo on your phone in your own voice..)

Create a space where you won't be bothered. Maybe light a candle, or burn some sage or palo santo to cleanse the energy, and play some soft meditation music at a hertz frequency you enjoy.

Find a comfortable position sitting or lying down with your neck straight, hands resting palms up, and close your eyes. Think about your intention for this past life journey – what do you want to clear, see, or understand? Or do you simply wish to observe what comes up?

Take a few deep belly breaths, allowing yourself to relax with each exhale. Feel your body sink into the ground, becoming heavier and more at ease.

Imagine a warm, golden light surrounding you, enveloping you in its protective glow. This light cleanses and purifies your energy field, dissolving any negative or stagnant energy. This light bubble is protecting you completely. We thank this bubble of light for its assistance.

Visualize an old heavy carved wooden door before you. This door is your gateway to your past lives. As you approach it, feel your intention to explore a significant past life that holds valuable insights for you today. Reach out and feel the wood on the door. Push the door open.

Take a deep breath and step through the doorway. You find yourself in a misty, soft realm. As the mist clears, your surroundings come into focus. Notice the details – what is the time period, the location, your appearance, and your role in this life?

"Who am I in this lifetime? What is happening to me? What am I doing in this lifetime?"

Allow the scene to unfold naturally. Observe the events, relationships, and experiences of this past life. Pay attention to any emotions, lessons, or patterns that feel significant.

Section I:

Questions to ask: *Why did this lifetime have to happen? What was the lesson? What belief was created in my dna that is not true? Is this belief or old program currently in this lifetime?*

As you explore this past life, be aware of any energetic imprints or attachments that no longer serve you. You might need to cry or scream or your body may shake. Whatever needs to be cleared, let it go.

Allow yourself to let go of anything no longer serving you. And so it is.

Now, visualize the golden light from earlier growing stronger, gently dissolving these outdated energies, beliefs or patterns. The golden light envelops you in love and truth, protection and guidance.

When you feel ready to return, thank this past life version of yourself for the insights gained. Thank the bubble of light for continuing to protect you today.

Step back through the door, carrying with you the wisdom and understanding you've received.

Back in the present, imagine roots growing from your feet deep into Gaia. Roots growing from your legs and root chakra down into the Mother. Feel yourself grounded and centered. We thank Mother Gaia for her love, support and guidance today and every day.

The golden light intensifies, forming a protective shield around you.

Take a moment to integrate the experience. Reflect on how the insights from this past life can positively influence your present and future.

Inner Work and Healing

When you're ready, slowly open your eyes, feeling refreshed, protected, and empowered. Thank yourself for going on this journey.

Remember to write down your experiences and insights in a journal (perhaps a past life journal ?).

You can do this meditation as many times as you wish to or as it calls to you. Most of us have between 10-100 lifetimes (sometimes many more!) which need to be cleared of energetic entanglements, false programming/outdated beliefs, wounds, etc. This can include lifetimes on this planet or on other planets, in other realms or dimensions, and in various life forms (*not just in human bodies!*).

We don't judge anything that comes up; we clear and integrate what is needed while we free whatever needs to go.

As you continue looking at your 'past lives', you might notice similar themes to this lifetime or similar relationships or partners, big paradigm shifts on other planets that you helped with, wars/battles for species and planets, and more. There is no right or wrong way to journey into your past lives. Find what works for you!

For other ways to clear, integrate and view past lives, please check out the free app <u>Insight Timer</u> and search 'past life healing' (it can also be referred to as checking and clearing your Akashic Records).

Choose one that you resonate with and know that if you try that one again, on a later day, it might not resonate. So you can try a different meditation for your continued journeying.

Here are a few that I've enjoyed:

Section 1:

- Past Life Regression Meditation by Trena Barnes - https://insig.ht/ZtYEb4hCuLb

- Past Life Regression Guided Meditation by Caroline Marie Jeanne - https://insig.ht/o9YdNJsCuLb

- Past Life Journey you're your Book of Records by Shannon Shine - https://insig.ht/z3wb3NoCuLb

- Clearing the Records by Joy Truscott - https://insig.ht/KxUUEgqCuLb

Wounds to specifically look at and ask to see the core wound or lifetime to clear. *All of these are heavy and intricate wounds, and might take multiple clearing sessions to find the root/core wound lifetime:*

mother wound, father wound,
divine mother wound, divine father wound, sisterhood and brotherhood wounds,
witch wound,
Atlantis wound, Lemuria wound,
separation from Source wound,
betrayal wound,
masculine wound, and feminine wound.

(This work can go faster if you have a trusted past life and timeline clearing energy healer assisting you.)

Step 7:
Developing Self-Sovereignty

Self-sovereignty is usually defined as the self-ownership over one's body, mind and spirit; that every person is autonomous in how they manage and operate their own knowledge, self, identity and life. Basically meaning that you have the ability to choose the direction of your life at all times, in any situation, and that it is your exclusive authority to do so.

I would say that all people on Gaia have struggled with a lack of self-sovereignty for many reasons (familial, societal, monetary etc.). Many are now embracing the idea of it; however the embodiment of it daily proves to be a journey in and of itself. Which is what we are totally here for, right?!

A few of the main factors that keep people from becoming (and maintaining) self-sovereignty are:

- Lack of self-confidence and self-love (especially inside of relationships)

- Low self-esteem and people pleasing

- Extreme empathy leading to self-abandonment

Section I:

- Minimal awareness of self-worth
- Unhealthy attachment styles
- Perfectionism and control

While we can look at the list above and say, "Nope, I'm good, I've healed all of that and I have no issues…" we can literally see it reflected in our outer world. The following questions might help you see where there is work to be done:

- Do you have exactly what your soul desires in all of your relationships?
- Do you feel valued and seen and heard?
- Do people give you the same amount of love, time and energy as you give them (in business, love and life)?
- Do you remain rooted in your values without being pushy about your beliefs?
- Do you take a leading coach/entrepreneur/business person/celebrity/personality's word for it, or do you feel if what they said is actually for you (in your body, your own knowing)?

In order to start the self-sovereignty journey, we can also look at the ego versus the higher self (the higher self is what we are integrating to remember our true state of being).

Honestly, all of the work in this book is to get you to return to your highest state of being and to integrate the ego as fully as possible in order to create a life from choices made through love (*versus fear, pain/hurt, avoidance, etc.*).

Review the picture below and be honest with yourself:

- What areas are not integrated?

- Where are you in your ego - what situations, around who, how are you feeling in your body when the ego gets control (*i.e. constantly tired, sick...*)?

- Are you always in an abundant mindset and grateful for everything?

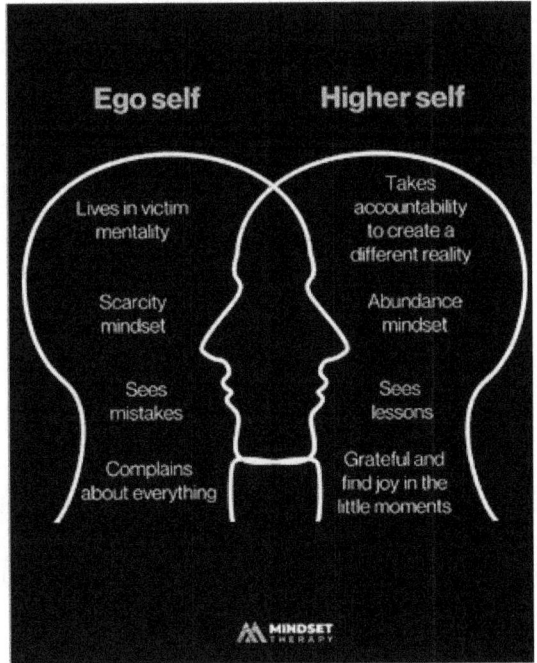

(https://www.instagram.com/mindset.therapy/p/CwlcbKcg00Q/)

First, let's start with the reflective areas to help shift your energy. Then we'll go onto daily mantras and practices.

Section I:

What is your attachment style?

Attachment styles refer to the ways in which humans form emotional bonds and relate to others, particularly in close relationships. These patterns are typically formed in early childhood based on interactions with primary caregivers, but they can influence relationships throughout our lives. Here's an overview of healthy and unhealthy attachment styles:

Healthy Attachment Style:

1. Secure Attachment:

- Characteristics: Trust, emotional openness, ability to give and receive support

- People with secure attachment feel comfortable with both intimacy and independence

- They have positive views of themselves and others

- They're able to communicate effectively and maintain healthy boundaries

Unhealthy Attachment Styles:

1. Anxious Attachment (also called Preoccupied):

- Characteristics: Fear of abandonment, need for constant reassurance

- These individuals often worry about their relationships and fear rejection

- They may become overly dependent on partners and struggle with self-worth

- They might engage in behaviors like constant texting or seeking excessive validation

2. Avoidant Attachment (also called Dismissive):

- Characteristics: Discomfort with emotional intimacy, and a strong sense of independence

- These individuals often suppress their feelings and avoid vulnerability

- They may prioritize their independence over relationships

- They might struggle to commit or may distance themselves when relationships become too close

3. Fearful-Avoidant Attachment (also called Disorganized):

- Characteristics: Conflicting desires for intimacy and fear of getting hurt

- These individuals often have experienced trauma or inconsistent caregiving

- They may simultaneously crave closeness and push others away

Section 1:

- Their behavior in relationships can be unpredictable and confusing

It's important to note that attachment styles exist on a spectrum, and most people may not fit perfectly into one category (usually 2-3 categories).

Moreover, with self-awareness and effort, it's possible to develop a more secure attachment style over time.

Developing a secure attachment style involves:

- Identifying your attachment patterns

- Working on self-esteem and self-worth

- Learning to communicate effectively

- Practicing emotional regulation (breathwork, yoga, qi-jong, etc.)

- Setting healthy boundaries

- Shadow work (see Step 4)

- Seeking therapy or counseling if needed

Understanding your attachment style can be a powerful tool for improving relationships and overall well-being. It can help you recognize patterns in your behavior and work towards forming healthier, more fulfilling connections with others.

Do you struggle for control?

Most of us have been programmed from an early age to maintain control at all times. Hide our emotions, don't be too loud, don't do this or that, take care of ourselves because nobody else will or give everything over to the care of a man/woman...there's a long list of generational programs that have been passed down by grandparents and parents from their own families.

What we must see is where we are trying to maintain control. When you look at all of your relationships, where have you tried to be seen a certain way, or show that you know more, or maintain the upper hand? Or where have you tried to always be there for everyone else but not letting anyone see your "weaknesses"? How many times a day do you try to prove to someone that your way of doing or thinking is the correct way?

If we are truly open with ourselves, we can see the tiny areas where we have allowed our egos to win and keep control - for a small victory that means nothing tomorrow.

These are a few questions to ask yourself:

- What relationships do I feel that I need to be in constant control or the loudest voice?

- What relationships do I feel unseen in?

- How do I look at my family members? Do I try to make them see my point of view or do I not engage with argumentative behavior?

Section 1:

- How do I perceive the most important women/men in my life? Do I accept them for who they are or do I keep trying to 'help' or change them?

- Do I allow my time to be taken up with things that I cannot change? Or am I willing to first work on my own internal thought processes, beliefs and programs in order to see the change outside of myself?

There is more than one way to let go of control. The more we stop trying to force a certain outcome (expectations are an energy drain!), the more we open ourselves up to the Divine flow and plan. We can move with more ease and grace versus feeling stuck, strain, rigid, or out of control.

It takes continual practice. How can you let go of control today?

Is your perfectionism killing your soul?

Perfectionism is usually formed in childhood, and not necessarily because your parents/caregivers expected it of you. It can also be an ingrained reaction when nothing was expected of you and/or you received minimal help, guidance and love from your parents.

However, it should be noted that perfectionism is known as the killer of relationships. And this includes the relationship you have with your own inner self.

The little signs of perfectionism can be seen in every area of life, whether it's having to get the perfect email sent out, or the perfect plan for a trip, or the perfect wedding day, or this or that...the perfection bug leaves no room for magic or mystery.

When we expect perfection in our own actions and what we produce, we expect it in others, disregarding the natural state of being human or allowances for the universe to bring in more magic. The stress and overwhelm that perfection requires, as side effects of its own unyielding rule, puts such an enormous strain on the nervous system. It's why we continue to see people burn out, become severely depressed and anxious, and simply not want to 'perform' anymore.

We must do better. But to do better, the change comes from within us. So how can you decide today that you no longer want to have these perfectionist tendencies? That you will embrace the natural ebbs and flows of all the wonder that is surrounding you in every moment of every day?

Do you have unhealthy or toxic relationships?

If every relationship you currently have is a reflection of you, how can this be keeping you in a holding pattern?

Many relationships we started years and years ago are no longer serving our highest good. We feel that we must be loyal to the person, yet they constantly complain or enjoy negative situations, or have refused to grow and learn new things.

When we have aligned with truth and continue developing our intuition (complete trust in our inner feminine), we can see where unhealthy relationships are and can protect ourselves from unhealthy/toxic/ dysfunctional relationships and people. Unfortunately, not everyone is aware of their own programs/ behaviors/traumas/wounds. It is not for us to point them out to

Section I:

others. It is only our responsibility about what we allow into our energy field, into our lives. What or who are we engaging with? Who are we letting into our energy and giving time to? Is unconditional love reciprocated?

In any situation, you can always ask your intuition, your heart, or your higher self if the person, place or thing is for your highest good or your highest alignment.

All of the questions above become second nature when we are rediscovering our self-sovereignty and aligning with our highest good.

Are you in your feminine power?

The majority of women lack confidence in their feminine power. There are various reasons for this but needless to say, we are responsible for accessing and loving our innate power.

Your feminine power is to be nurturing, intuitive, creative and receptive. Yes, we give love but we also open up wider to receive it. We are highly spiritual beings and the more we can connect with our own feminine aspect, the more balanced we feel within ourselves.

These questions can assist your reflection:

- How can you feel more confident in your feminine power?

- How do you nurture yourself first (*even if it's only 10 minutes of meditation or breathwork*), then take care of others?

- What have you created lately (*art, music, food, a clean house...*)?

- Are you open to receiving from the masculine (*inner and outer*)?

- What relationships have you been masculine in, and which are you currently more feminine in?

Simply being aware of our own subtle inclinations (depending on the situation and person) can help us see where we might feel we need to slip into a more 'appropriate' or old pattern.

Each one of us is in this process together – this reclamation of true feminine essence. Stay gentle with yourself and trust in the unfolding as you blossom into the wonderful being you have always been (because it is your soul truth!).

Daily Practices:

Self-Esteem Daily Practice - a combination of mental, emotional, and physical activities. Here's a comprehensive daily routine that can help boost self-esteem:

1. Morning affirmations: Start your day with positive self-talk. Look in the mirror and say affirmations like:

    - "I am worthy of love and respect"

    - "I am capable and strong"

    - "I embrace my unique qualities"

2. Gratitude journaling: Write down three things you're grateful for about yourself each day. Focus on your positive attributes.

Section I:

- Self-care ritual: Dedicate time each day for self-care, whether it's a skincare routine, a relaxing bath, or simply taking a few deep breaths.

- Physical exercise: Engage in some form of physical activity daily. This could be yoga, a walk, dance, or any exercise you enjoy. Physical activity boosts mood and confidence.

- Mindfulness or meditation: Practice being present and non-judgmental. This can help reduce negative self-talk and increase self-awareness.

- Skill development: Spend time each day (if possible) learning or practicing a skill. This could be related to a hobby, career, or personal interest. Continuous learning boosts confidence.

- Boundary setting: Practice saying "no" to things that don't align with your values or drain your energy. Respect your own needs and limits.

- Positive social connections: Reach out to a friend or a loved one at least a few times per week. Nurture relationships that are supportive and uplifting.

- Self-compassion practice: When you make a mistake or face a challenge, practice self-compassion. Treat yourself with the kindness you'd offer a good friend.

- Celebrate small wins: At the end of each day, acknowledge and celebrate your accomplishments, no matter how small. Write down 1 daily.

- Dress for success: Wear clothes that make you feel confident and comfortable, even if you're staying at home.

- Positive media consumption: Be mindful of the media you consume. Choose content that inspires and uplifts you rather than making you feel inadequate.

- Evening reflection: Before bed, reflect on positive moments from your day and how you embodied your values.

- Visualization: Visualize yourself succeeding in your goals and feeling confident.

- Body appreciation: Each day, acknowledge something you appreciate about your body's functionality rather than just its appearance.

🌱Creating a daily mantra for yourself. Here is a sample mantra (*write your mantra down on a sticky note or piece of paper to say joyfully to yourself out loud every day for the next 21+ days*):

Today, I give thanks for my many blessings and opportunities. I will express my emotions as they come up to be seen and heard, and I will be kind to my neighbor and every living thing.

I surrender myself to you, God/The Divine/Source. I surrender to the Divine Plan. I appreciate your guidance and I trust in you.

I am here, I am here, I am here. I am free, I am free, I am free!

Section I:

🌹<u>Self-Care Practice:</u> Take time for you. Find something you truly care about that you will do every day. Whether it's a skincare routine in the morning, a relaxing salt bath at night, dry brushing and lymphatic massage 2-3 times per week, or simply taking a few deep breaths, make self-care a priority for 10 minutes per day.

🌹<u>Loving Kindness Mediation:</u> Every night, or whenever you are not feeling very loving or have had a trying day, practice a loving kindness meditation where you direct loving energy towards yourself first. After you feel this love towards yourself for 2-3 minutes, you can direct it towards others or to the world at large.

Section II:
Clearing Blocks

Section II:

In this section, we will focus on clearing even deeper blocks to your internal union. This is integral work here and it will allow you to shift faster. Most of these practices need to be done continuously for a minimum of 3 months, until they are a habit.

Please check in with yourself every 6 months because the ego has a habit of telling us we do not need to do anymore work in the area, or we've healed it completely, or there's nothing deeper to look at. It's important to understand that we can cry or scream over a memory, wound or block that we have previously worked on, and to be gentle on ourselves for whatever needs to happen on this journey.

Some of the biggest blocks for Inner Union are: Forgiveness, Worthiness, Inner Child Relationship, and Feminine Embodiment and Receiving. I will be going over all of these in more detail in the coming pages.

Take the practice that resonates the most with you and go further with it – *make it your own!*

Practice 1:
Releasing Attachments

The ties that bind us in this reality are both seen and unseen. Maintaining a clear energy is of utmost importance, not only for our own energy field but also in order to consciously create (manifest) our soul desires. The more we are able to let go of what no longer serves us, the more our energy creates space. The more space created in our energy field, the more we are able to receive -> love, abundance, gratitude, money...everything!

The most common energy tie that holds people back is their past relationships or current relationships they allow themselves to be treated less than, past sexual partners, and past life relationships. Due to karma, we have relationships in this lifetime with partners from previous lifetimes where we did not learn the lesson. The majority of relationships currently are these repeated karmic relationships. Which means they are not of your highest alignment or highest timeline (however you want to refer to your highest good).

First, we must get honest with ourselves. Who is still around - lingering in our energy field, subconscious or dreams? Perhaps you have someone on the 'back burner' in case your person never shows up? Maybe you constantly think about 'the one that got away'? Or do you dream about your first/second/third love repeatedly most weeks?

Section II:

We will start with a list. Answer these as truthfully as you can. Try to penetrate through any excuses or fantasies.

1. Who have I wronged in any partner or lover relationship(s)? Who in my friends and family have I wronged?

   _____

   _____

2. Who has wronged me?

   _____

   _____

3. What resentments do I still hold about men/women based on this past relationship(s)? *Simply by acknowledging any lingering emotions about past partners without any judgment is how we are able to clear it out of our energy field.*

   _____

   _____

4. What did I project onto them?

   _____

   _____

5. What did they project onto me?

   _____

6. Am I ready to truly liberate them from my energy, my mind, my body?

7. If so, write a letter (on a separate sheet of paper) to each person who still lingers in your thoughts, energy, dreams... Stream this letter – let out everything you ever felt, thought, any negative emotions, anything unresolved, etc. *Allow yourself to cry, scream, punch a pillow, or whatever your body wants to do to let go.*

8. Ask your higher self if this person was a karmic relationship or lesson? Write down on the sheet anything that comes to you (feelings, sensations, memories, visions, tastes...)

9. Ask your higher self if there is anything else that needs to be cleared regarding this person in this lifetime or any other.

Section II:

10. Once everything has been written down, go to a safe space and burn the letter or tear it up entirely - and scatter it in the wind (or trash).

11. Recite this affirmation for 14 days: "I let go of the past with love and open myself to new possibilities."

12. Do any shaking exercise or heart-opening yoga poses to move any stagnant energy from these completed past relationships.

13. Practice a self-loving ritual such as taking a warm bath or giving yourself a massage with essential oils like lavender, frankincense or ylang-ylang.

14. While looking in the mirror, into your own eyes, say out loud, "I am so grateful now that I have let go of this old energy. I love you enough to move forward to my highest timeline. Thank you, thank you, thank you for helping me do this and for being you!"

_____

_____

Now, let's go even deeper into our past projections in relationships to understand if we have cleared them fully from our programming (subconscious behaviors or outdated beliefs learned in childhood).

Projections are unconscious psychological processes where individuals attribute their own thoughts, feelings, or traits onto others. In unhealthy relationships, these projections can be particularly damaging.

Here's a list of common types of projections in unhealthy/dysfunctional relationships:

1. Insecurity Projection:

- Projecting one's own insecurities onto the partner

- Example: A person who is insecure about their appearance constantly accuses their partner of finding others attractive

2. Guilt Projection:

- Attributing one's own feelings of guilt to the partner

- Example: A cheating partner accusing the other of infidelity without evidence

3. Anger Projection:

- Projecting unresolved anger onto the partner

- Example: Someone with repressed anger from childhood lashing out at their partner over minor issues

4. Fear of Abandonment Projection:

- Projecting fears of being left onto the partner

- Example: Constantly accusing the partner of planning to leave, even when there's no indication

5. Responsibility Projection:

- Projecting one's own responsibilities or failures onto the partner

- Example: Blaming the partner for one's own career setbacks or personal shortcomings

6. Idealization Projection:

- Projecting an idealized image onto the partner, setting unrealistic expectations

- Example: Expecting the partner to fulfill all roles (friend, lover, therapist, etc.) perfectly

7. Shadow Projection:

- Projecting disowned parts of oneself (the "shadow") onto the partner

- Example: A person who suppresses their own anger or aggression constantly accuses their partner of being "too aggressive" or "always angry," even in situations where the partner's reactions are reasonable or justified.

8. Control Projection:

- Projecting one's own need for control onto the partner

- Example: Accusing the partner of being controlling while actually being the controlling one

9. Emotional Unavailability Projection:

- Projecting one's own emotional distance onto the partner

- Example: Accusing the partner of being cold or unfeeling when one is actually emotionally unavailable

10. Past Trauma Projection:

- Projecting unresolved issues from past relationships onto the current partner

- Example: Treating the current partner with distrust due to a previous partner's infidelity

11. Self-Worth Projection:

Section II:

- Projecting one's own self-esteem issues onto the partner

- Example: Constantly seeking validation and accusing the partner of not valuing or loving them enough

12. Perfectionism Projection:

- Projecting unrealistic standards onto the partner

- Example: Criticizing the partner for minor flaws while ignoring one's own imperfections

Do any of these projections above come up for you in any way?

If yes, let's see the situation and forgive ourselves for behaving that way at that time (a past version of self) and commit to not doing that again in the future.

If any of these are happening to you in your current partner relationship, ask yourself if this is a situation you deserve or want to stay in (at a soul level)? As you are not responsible for changing another person, the answer can be felt in your body and in your heart.

What do you truly desire in your inner and outer relationships?

If any of these projections are happening in other relationships (family, friends, mentors, coworkers, etc.), this is based on an old version of you as well. Are you ready to insert your boundaries and uphold them? Are you ready to show yourself the respect and love that you know you deserve?

You are the only one who can change your situation. Yes, change begins within us. But sometimes, we have to change our situation, leave our current environment, in order to create the life we truly desire and be surrounded by more loving, higher consciousness people, places and things.

Ho'oponopono

If you are unsure of what attachments might be lingering in the background or in your subconscious, there is a practice that can detach cords and attachments quickly.

Ho'oponopono is an ancient Hawaiian practice that heals ourselves, relationships and others, as well as allows for the movement of stagnant energy out of our bodies. It is the practice of reconciliation and forgiveness, and was primarily used in Hawaiian culture for resolving family issues.

When you feel stuck, heavy, or know that you have something you need to let go of, but are unsure of what "it" is, this is a great practice to do.

First, do this for yourself.

Then, do it for anyone who you feel lingering emotions about, such as guilt, shame, sadness, grief, rejection, abandonment, etc. Maybe a relationship is strained or was left behind, or perhaps you feel guilty about how you behaved or didn't do something for someone. *You can also use this for a client, family member, or friend who is going through a really difficult time as this follows the mirror belief that everything externally comes from our own internal state...* We hold all of these unexpressed emotions within our body and when we

Section II:

repeat this prayer, it clears all that needs to go in regards to the person or situation.

Energetically speaking, it heals all wounds related to this person or situation and clears the karma related to it.

1. **Sit down** in a comfortable seated position where you will not be disturbed and can speak out loud, and cry or grieve whatever comes up.

2. **Place a picture** of yourself (or the other person) in front of you. If you are great at visualization, see yourself or the other person in your mind's eye. You will focus on this picture while you say the prayer.

3. **Say out loud** in repetition for 5 minutes, "I am sorry. Please forgive me. Thank you. I love you."

4. Allow whatever comes up - tears, sobs, etc.- to be moved out of your body. This is the healing and energy clearing.

Practice 2:
Forgiveness

Forgiveness, of self and others, is another thing we are not taught to truly do as a child. We hold resentments and grudges; we are sensitive and we are wounded so deeply by our caregivers and the people we thought were here to love us. And then, we turn that wounding upon ourselves because we feel that we are the problem, people will love us if we change and do what they tell (and show) us to do.

So we hide our soul away and put massive walls up around our hearts, hurting ourselves even further in the process.

Yet, we are choosing a different way to BE now. We are choosing to continue to heal and clear what must be freed in order to come into our inner union.

A big part of this work is to take a look at where we do not forgive ourselves. Where do we belittle ourselves for a past 'mistake' (learning lesson) or past relationship? Where are we not remembering that we did the best we could with the knowledge and level of embodiment we had at the time the event occurred?

How can we forgive ourselves truly and wholeheartedly?

Section II:

Here are some practices to take this work deeper. Be gentle with yourself. Tears and grief will most likely come up. Sit with the emotions and let them go – allow them to flow through you.

Forgiveness Practices:

1. Think of one event/memory that has recently come into your awareness where you felt someone crossed a boundary and really hurt you. *This can be around your self-worth, self-love or any other false programming that occurred after this event happened.*

2. Try to truly forgive the person who did this to you but understand that forgiveness can take time and is a process.

3. Write them a letter if verbalizing the forgiveness isn't working. Really allow your inner child to let it out! Have at them. Express the rage or fear you felt, etc.

List what you did to others or how you hurt them (manipulation, abuse, etc.) throughout your life. Be very honest.

Did you lie to someone in the past that it still haunts you?

Did you cheat or abuse even though that's not who you truly are?

Did you stay in a relationship you knew was not good for you?

Do you commit to no longer doing this?

Work on forgiving yourself for these past actions and understand it's a process to truly forgive yourself and your past behaviors that were stemming from your trauma.

- Write a letter to yourself (at that time period of your life) and say everything to her you want her to know. Allow her to speak and then give her a hug. Tell her you are proud of her and look how far you have come!

_____

_____

_____

_____

_____

_____

_____

_____

_____

_____

_____

Section II:

Practice 3:
Worthiness

Most of us have done some form of self-worth work to get to where we are now. Treating ourselves worthy of having what our soul desires is an ongoing process, and with each new level that we come to, there can be more to clear or deeper levels to heal.

Unfortunately, our parents never taught us to feel worthy of being here simply because they never felt or learned that themselves. Sometimes, a narcissist parent can project worthiness feelings outwardly but it is to cover deeper wounding. We are speaking here about at the core of our very being, do we feel worthy enough of our soul's desires?

We tend to make bargains with ourselves – "when I get to this point or achieve this thing, I'll reward myself with that dress or that trip or ____". This thinking shows us that we don't believe that we are inherently worthy of having, doing or being the thing we truly desire until we have done something to prove that we are worthy of it. It's a slippery slope with this because the ego loves this game!

So first, ask yourself, when will you feel worthy enough to have what you truly desire (your person/counterpart showing up, a successful business, losing ____ amount of weight)?

Is this the point that you believe in your subconscious that you're good enough to be loved - once you've achieved ____?

When you say to yourself (*try this while looking at yourself in the mirror, into your own eyes*), "I am worthy of love even though I'm not making $____ months or don't have a thriving business or my person hasn't shown up yet, etc., I love myself as I am."

How did that feel in your body when you said that? What part of your body didn't feel it or contracted or tightened up?

If you felt the contracting in your body, you don't believe that you love yourself as you are right in this moment, that you are worthy of what you desire just because you are alive.

We can go through all of the cultural/societal rules of conditional love. Most of us grew up in these settings and we learn to stay safe, that we must settle or allow what we don't truly desire, and because this programming carries over into adulthood, we continue settling or allowing in all areas - relationships, business, pricing, living situations, health and weight...

Yet every time that you settle or allow, you don't feel worthy and you reinforce the programming of unworthiness.

An example of settling is that if it doesn't light you up with a feeling of "hell yeah!", it's a NO!

If it's a wishy-washy maybe, it's a NO. If it's second-guessing your first instinct or gut feeling, it's a NO. If it's a 'God, this is going to make it so much harder for myself if I allow this to happen - but it'll make it easier for them', it's an absolute NO.

Section II:

We don't settle or people please to make it easier for everyone else, making ourselves suffer because of that choice or action. We say NO to the energy of settling (*this doesn't include a transition period when the residual energy is being cleared*).

Clearing Blocks

Worthiness Practice

Practice every day and week until it becomes a habit
(*21 days minimum*).
Use a separate journal or sheets of paper.

1. What are your true desires from your heart/soul for your relationships? For your business/job? For your health/body?

   _____

   _____

2. Do you truly know what you really want? *(For example, I only want to work 20 hours per week so that I can escort my kids to their activities and school. Or I don't work on my moon/period and my business is based around that so that I can focus on myself..)*

   _____

   _____

3. Can you feel it in your body, does it bring you pleasure (yes, in your yoni/womb)?

   _____

   _____

(i.e. I desire to be nurtured and satisfied with my creative or healing work; to be loved and appreciated by my family or partner; to live in a house that feels high vibrational and joyful.)

Section II:

Now that you've understood your soul desires for this moment in time, I'm going to talk about the energetic alignment of giving and receiving abundantly.

It's very similar to how we say hell no to things that are not for us. We say "hell yes!" to aligned things that bring us pleasure (this can be felt in the sacral/womb or the solar plexus) and a "hell no" to things that feel off or negative.

When you live in this manner of really listening to your body about what is an absolute YES or an absolute NO, you will receive more.

It's that simple - and that hard because we weren't programmed this way from childhood. We were taught to deny our light, to deny what we truly wanted or didn't want, to give hugs to people we cringed from, to say hi to weirdos because they were our parent's friends, etc.

So when you honor your "YES!" and your "NO!", you honor your soul truth. Your body. Your feelings. You honor what you need in that moment and you respect yourself enough to uphold that YES or NO.

Which brings us to the alignment practice.

Alignment Practice for Worthiness

Practice this daily and weekly until it is a habit
(*21 days minimum*).
Use a separate sheet of paper.

Sit down in a quiet space, take 3 deep belly breaths, and ask yourself:

1. What feels off or is draining my energy?

   _____

   _____

2. What gives me the most energy or feels good in my body to do? *Your body knows the truth.*

   _____

   _____

3. What are the top 3 things I desire today? (*i.e. I want to go for a hike. I desire to ecstatic dance. I want to buy that silk dress.*)

   _____

   _____

Now, let's reframe what settling does in our system. What you settle for today cuts down the time on being where you truly want to be. When you settle for that thing with "ugh, I guess, okay fine", you are pushing out a higher timeline and your true soul desires.

Section II:

For example, when you settle for dating that guy that you know isn't your Divine Counterpart (because he brings drama or chaos and is filled with trauma), you push away your higher timeline of your true person showing up. The longer you settle for this other guy, the longer you delay your soul desire of your Counterpart.

It's the same for a job or your soul clients - if you settle for that job you know pays you less for your work or for clients who aren't fully aligned to your work (or who want you to do all the work instead of them doing anything), then you push your true soul aligned job or soul aligned clients away from you. The universe doesn't respond to what we desire unless we are matching the vibration of what we desire. It doesn't care about your words - it only responds to your actions/your energy. If you are repeatedly showing the universe that you will take bread crumbs, it will continue giving you bread crumbs.

Because that "settling for bread crumbs" energy is unworthiness energy.

Which brings up the questions - would you feel worthy of your desires if they showed up right now? If you received $20,000 right now from out of nowhere, would you feel worthy of it? If you ran into your person in the grocery store, would you feel worthy of him (or think he was above your league)? If you were given a compliment, would you say "thank you" or would you shrug it off or try to give it back/return it with a compliment?

Would you be able to FEEL and SEE what came to you and receive it with gratitude, love and grace? Or would you be blind to it because you don't feel truly worthy of it?

If you FEEL worthy of your soul's desire, it shows up. It is UNIVERSAL LAW. Our internal energetic vibration is what shows up in our reality.

Because this work is so multilayered, it's good to start with a solid foundation and habit. Here are a few exercises to get you going.

Self-Worth Exercises

- If you feel you aren't worthy of money, love, abundance, etc., more shadow work and energy healing is required. We need to move the self-worth feelings from "I can only have something when I do something" to "**I am good enough to do/buy/have that now.**" See the shadow work section in this workbook or check out energy healing meditations on self-worth.

- Speaking to your inner child, visualizing or feeling her show up, and telling her daily: "You are worthy of love just as you are and I love you so much!" Giving her a huge hug helps too!

- Saying to yourself in the mirror daily: "**I am inherently valuable because I exist**" until you feel the belief within you.

- Rewiring your brain to KNOW that the Divine Feminine is the BEing (and the Divine Masculine is the DOing). That she is worthy just because she is alive! That the feminine state of nurturing, unconditional love and peace energy elevates our man, our family, our kids, just by BEing. "**In this moment, I choose to embody my Divine Feminine and I am worthy to simply BE.**"

- Notice where you undercharge for your time, services, or any energy exchange. Undercharging creates resentment. In any job or business or offering, find the energetic alignment for every service and price point. What is your true soul worth? *Feel/See where there is any resistance to charging your worth,*

Section II:

raising your prices per your guidance system, or asking for a raise or leaving your current job for a higher paying one.

- Asking yourself: where have I over-delivered or over-given at the expense of my own self (people pleasing). *How can you create boundaries around that and uphold your self-worth to not do it again?*

- Where have people crossed your boundaries lately? Where are you being tested to uphold your boundaries or firm them up? Has it been in business/job, with friends and family, with clients? *Where do you need to say "NO" instead of trying to make others happy?*

- When are you triggered into feeling the need to earn or hustle to get what you want? Do you feel triggered when your bank account is low or when you haven't been on a date in months? *Notice where you feel that you need to earn worthiness, money, love, etc.*

- Ask yourself: Is there anywhere else in my life where this pattern is being reflected so that I can heal it? Where don't I feel worthy? Exposing it all helps to bring it to the light to heal it.

- Where have you said, "I don't have enough for what I truly desire" because that is the energetic vibration of I don't believe I'm enough.

Practice 4:
Inner Child

The inner child can show up in various ages when we start to connect with her. It is very valuable to see her wherever she wants to show up on that day and continue to speak with her and encourage her.

She is a neglected aspect of our being and that is what we are remedying today.

It starts with the willingness to say that you see her and love her, and to also become dedicated to building up your relationship with her.

If she doesn't trust you, ask why? Find out how you can help her trust you. What do you need to do for yourself in your life to build that trust?

When she shows up as a teenager, allow her to tell you about all of her woes and fears and everything. She needed a healthy adult and you are the only one that she can count on.

This inner child work is also called "reparenting". You are reparenting yourself in the way that you wished you had been parented as a

Section II:

child and teenager - with unconditional love, honor and respect, encouragement and fun, laughter and joy.

On the way to that unconditional relationship, we must remove all of the stuck emotions, memories and false programs so that your inner child feels free, heard/seen, and consistently loved!

Inner Child Practice:

Connect to your inner child and give her love every day. IF this is the only thing that you do for 21 days, it will still make massive changes in your life!

1. Sitting in a quiet space where you won't be disturbed (phone off!).

    _____

    _____

2. Calling in your inner child (this will be a specific age, and multiple ages can come in at once to clear).

    _____

    _____

3. Taking 1 minute to tell her everything she needed to hear when she was little (everything that you needed to hear as a baby, child, teen). Give her unconditional love, value her, and tell her that her desires and dreams are valid. That they are

beautiful and you are proud of her for her dreams and desires – for voicing them and knowing that they will happen!

_____

_____

4. Do this every day for 21 days and see the shifts!

_____

_____

Asking her every day (or every few to start) what she would like to do today, and seeing how she responds also helps her start to trust you. She will understand that you want her to be happy and joyful the more she is allowed to express herself in various ways of play, creation, art, etc.

Making her a priority will shift your life. The more you can connect with her, the deeper your relationship with her will grow. She wants to help you fulfill the dreams you both hold, she wants to give you love as you give her love. Your inner child can create havoc in your life if she feels neglected, disregarded or unwanted. For example, she can start playing with other people's wounded inner child or shadows if she feels ignored or unloved – which brings these people into your life and can also cause drama, traumatization, or hard lessons.

The more that you can connect with her (through meditation, through the exercise above, through drawing or play or fun, etc.), the more she will help you create your soul desires because she is an aspect of your soul in this lifetime.

Section II:

Practice 5:
Your Inner Feminine and Receiving

Our inner feminine aspect is something we must engage with until she is fully integrated into our being on this planet.

There were two ways that most of us grew up – being forced into our lower masculine via competition and survival in the patriarchal system, or being forced into our lower feminine via helplessness and victimhood/ martyrdom. Usually this was what we saw our mothers do, and we mirrored it from a young age. As we grew older, we had some form of breakdown(s) of that old way of being until we became ready to hold the true feminine codes – the Divine Feminine.

Natural feminine energy is receiving, which means we have to allow ourselves to open up and receive (*instead of the old way of saying 'No' to help, money, relationships, etc.*). When I say allow, I mean give yourself permission to open up and to receive. Open up here means to clear enough stagnant energy and outdated beliefs/systems/ programs buried in your subconscious and human brain that you are able to make more space to, and become ready to, receive the new (*ideas, thoughts, beliefs, ways of doing or being...*) that wants to come to you.

Clearing Blocks

The feminine energy is not just creation (new ideas, new life, new art, etc). She is also the receiver. Structure and strategy is masculine energy while the feminine receives. This is the true blueprint of the Divine Feminine, instead of the old system of constantly giving, showing up, feeling exhausted and overwhelmed, in a perpetual state of busy-ness, etc.

To explore this further, let's begin to look at the state your inner feminine is in.

Sit in a place where you won't be disturbed. Take out a few sheets of paper and take three big, deep belly breaths, in and out of your nose. Calm your system. Now place your hand on your heart and ask your inner feminine to step forward, that you would like to ask her some questions.

Note her answers down on the sheet of paper.

1. Is she ready to receive?

   _____

   _____

   _____

2. Does she feel worthy enough to receive?

   _____

   _____

   _____

Section II:

3. Have the outdated beliefs holding me back (*in finances, home, relationship, work, etc.*) been deleted and are the new ones ready to flow through you, through your channel and your vessel?

_____

_____

_____

4. Are you ready to embody your feminine fully?

_____

_____

_____

5. What else needs to clear or be let go of that I can clear today?

_____

_____

_____

After you have listened to these answers and done as your inner feminine has guided you, it's time to dive even deeper into this feminine piece.

Ask your inner feminine:

1. Does my business/career/work support you, my inner feminine? Or am I constantly producing and working and being pushed into my masculine?

   _____

   _____

2. Do I wake up feeling nourished and motivated, in my brilliance and genius? Or do I get right to work, forcing and pushing for my outcomes?

   _____

   _____

3. Where am I in my feminine and where am I in masculine with:

   _____

   _____

   a. money,

   b. business/job/career,

   c. health,

   d. partner/spouse

   e. friendships,

   f. home/living situation,

   g. anything else you want to ask about.

Section II:

4. Do my personal relationship(s) support me and are every one of them in equal energy exchange – meaning there is equal give and take?

_____

_____

Notice your answers here and see any unhealthy patterns or cycles that need to be ended. Your commitment to ending these patterns is why you came here at this time – these cycles end with you in your earthly bloodline. They are also assisting the planet with higher levels of consciousness and your own soul journey through these lessons.

The biggest issues around being able to receive, from what I have seen with clients and my own path, always comes down to certain behaviors that stem from codependency and traumatic childhood. We can say that these come from past lives on this planet and are compounded in this lifetime for us to clear, but for now, we will focus on this lifetime's issues.

Issues around receiving:

- Feeling undeserving or downplaying/ not expressing needs to self or others,

- Feeling guilt and discomfort when someone wants to buy you something or compliment you, and deflecting compliments ("*Oh this dress, I just got it from TK Maxx.*"),

- Overcompensating when you've received (*with thanks/ gratitude or in business with giving away your time after payment*),

- Hard time receiving help (*"I'll just do it myself."*),

- Resisting rest (*not allowing yourself to receive rest or allowing your body to rest*),

- Not prioritizing your rest (*not working on your period, not verbalizing needs of rest to others*),

- Not allowing your emotions to take up space or even acknowledging them (*cannot verbalize or voice how you feel or avoid asking yourself how you feel today*),

- Avoiding feeling emotions (*"I hate crying so I just don't", "I don't want to feel this way", etc.*),

- People pleasing (*the opposite of Divine Feminine is prioritizing others above self*),

- Over-sacrifice/over-giving and being a martyr (see *mother wound*),

- Fear of abandonment or rejection,

- Low self-worth,

- Codependency - giving away or outsourcing your power,

- Suppressed soul desires - afraid of expressing your true desires,

Section II:

- Lack of boundaries - reframe with affirmations such as: "*My bank account <u>is always above</u> $10,000*", or "*I only allow equal, supportive and unconditionally loving relationships in my reality.*" Or "*I accept an overflowing avalanche of money*", etc.,

- Jealousy and/or comparison - no love or respect for self and inherent gifts, skills and service,

- Neglecting self by "pushing through" despite your body's needs -> can receive a bit in this wounded feminine state but not a lot or overflow.

Understanding where you have any of the issues above to receiving will help you pinpoint what old beliefs or patterns can be cleared. Then you can start reprogramming yourself to higher programs of wealth, abundance, prosperity, etc.

That is when we step out of the wounded feminine who has issues receiving, and into our truth, the Divine Feminine who is overflowing abundance and love.

Emotions

When we suppress our emotions, which is a trait we usually learned in childhood, we are not allowing the emotions to flow through our bodies. Therefore, we hold onto those emotions, and truly, we can experience hundreds, if not thousands, of emotions in a single day. We bury these emotions in our hips, our joints, our wombs…anywhere that can hold more suppressed emotions gets more added on, year by year, compounding on top of what we already have stored throughout our entire lives.

I'm not only talking about the big traumatic experiences here, I'm also speaking on the small interactions with others that we have much more of in our current realities. This can be a stranger ramming into you at the grocery store and not saying sorry, or a nasty comment on one of your social media posts, or a friend misunderstanding your reaction or words. When we don't understand our feelings in real time, we stuff them down and down and pretend they don't exist, or that the incident was so small that you shouldn't be affected by it.

Yet to be human is to have emotions. To experience our feelings. To have human connection, which means there will always be emotions involved – this is also what we came here to live. We love this planet and we love the lessons we learn here, as well as eating amazing, nourishing food or sleeping on the softest, most luxurious bed ever!

However, due to the societal and religious connotations with negative emotions - such as shame, jealousy, guilt, anger - we are taught to suppress them and not show them or let them out. Even as a child, you are taught not to throw a tantrum so that you don't embarrass your parents – when you were probably either exhausted and needed a nap (so not allowed to rest!) or you were picking up on someone else's energy of anger/frustration and were trying to move it out of your body (usually we process our parent's stuffed emotions as children, or we try to before we're programmed not to show emotions).

So let's reprogram our brains and our subconscious that these so-called "negative" emotions are actually warning signs (aka triggers) and are here to help us! It's our body's way of alerting us that something is off.

Section II:

These 'negative' emotions (*guilt, anger, shame, resentment, frustration, jealousy/envy, etc.*) are showing us that there is something more to clear or heal within ourselves. Or that someone has crossed a boundary and our body is saying "No!"

When we are able to let the emotion guide us - to show us what needs to be seen - and then allow the emotion to flow through us so that we aren't holding onto it anymore, we have mastered emotional flow.

There is one other area to be aware of with emotions and that is we pick up on the energies of others - even if we protect our energy all of the time. We can still take on other people's stuff consciously and subconsciously.

If it's someone else's emotions that you are holding or experiencing (*ask your body if the emotion you are feeling is actually yours*), you get to let it go easier. See/feel the emotion, say "Thank you for coming up to be cleared" and then let it go. It's not yours to carry. It is similar to how we remove energy cords and densities from others, and send them back with unconditional love.

We can love our emotions - all of them - by feeling unconditional love towards ourselves, allowing ourselves to experience all of the emotions that we are capable of (as humans). And then to let them go once they have been seen/heard.

This is the same with rest and our own energy. **The more we give to ourselves** (*by prioritizing our own self*)**, the more we shift the energy and can receive more.**

And when I say receive more, it can be about overflow as well. We must reprogram ourselves to <u>believe</u> in abundance. For example, if you write your book or craft posts/content or create art for 2 hours, what you receive from that work is far more than the hours you put in. Abundance is to believe that equal energy exchange is the bare minimum you will receive. Yes, even with your soul clients or purpose work.

If you are doing your soul work and acting on all you are guided to do (*from your teams, your highest self, the higher self of your book/ offer/job/art/ children/etc.*), you will be in a state of overflow. Why? Because you are aligned to your highest timeline, your highest state. Your soul purpose 'work' doesn't feel like work; it is literally what you came here to do. You are abundantly provided for because you are performing your service to the highest good of yourself and this planet.

This soul purpose alignment is also something to tap into with your inner feminine – that she is being fully expressed in your work and your life. Her dreams and creations are fulfilled by the inner masculine. He is the do-er.

Divine Masculine Assistance

Our inner masculine's deepest desire is to help our inner feminine live her deepest desires. He craves seeing her happy, thriving and loving life!

This is where understanding his role comes in.

Section II:

Taking divinely guided action steps to create provision for the divine feminine is the role of the divine masculine. He creates all of the healthy boundaries, pillars, structures, and systems for implementing whatever it is that she desires to create/birth.

The feminine loves structure in order to help her be more in her feminine energy - because she knows what's happening and why. She knows why the structure is in place. However, she does NOT enjoy creating the structure. That's her masculine counterpart's job.

And that's what he loves to do.

For example, the feminine will say something such as, "This month, I want to create a book about ____."

In response, the masculine says, "Alright, my love. I will block off 3 days a week on your calendar for 5 hours to sit and write for the next 3 weeks. We will move all of your clients to 2 days each week, and we will give you 2 full rest days. Then we will allow your period week at the end of the month. We will schedule all of your posts so that you aren't thinking about that and you can focus on writing."

He has now created the structure using his systems (for posting, clients, etc.) for her to have the space to write her book.

Now she can relax and write!

<u>The more there is structure and systems to business, career, and finances, the more the feminine will relax, thrive and create</u>. Without these, she flounders, feels lost and feels unprotected. However, she must have the soul-led clarity and direction (her true desires) to give to the masculine so that he can then take action.

Wounding

All of this inner feminine receiving can be hindered by deep wounds. If these wounds are unexamined and cleared, they remain in the subconscious. Sometimes these wounds are from this lifetime, sometimes they are from other lifetimes.

Here is a list of wounds that will need to be brought to the light and healed, with an understanding that some of these (if not all) are similar to peeling an onion. They are layer upon layer and sometimes we forget about them until we are triggered into a deeper level of healing them by an event or situation.

- **Mother and Father Wounds** - for example your Father wound (with Gaia ly dad) - shows up in your relationship with money and business. Is money consistent in your life and business? Or is it hiding or you never know when it's showing up? If this is the case, more inner work on this is necessary.

- **Sisterhood Wounds** - we see this commonly as betrayals, being taken advantage of (used), or discarded/rejected. This shows up in relationships with women.

- **Brotherhood Wounds** (mostly past lives) - this shows up in mistrust of men and warring/control mentality.

- **Womb and Yoni Wounds** - the more trauma that your womb or yoni has experienced, the more it will repel men, money, business, etc. until it feels completely safe in its depths.

- **Heart wounds** - this shows more with heart pains or palpitations. This can be a sign of distrusting your own heart, or your own guidance. Work on strengthening your relationship with your heart/yourself - this is required for your inner union. *If this happens when others are around, ask your heart who she doesn't feel safe with.*

Divine Feminine Traits

In order to reframe and to heal, it's important for us to understand exactly what it means to say you are a Divine Feminine completely embodied. There are certain characteristics and traits that you carry within you because you are DIVINE. You are directly connected to Source.

This means you are a Divine Feminine incarnate; this is your natural state of Being.

Yet, the lifetimes we have lived on this planet and in other realms and realities has sometimes taken chunks out of us. By the time we got to this lifetime, and since we didn't witness a Divine Feminine around us growing up, we forgot our natural state. It was programmed out of us.

Below are traits that you innately have within you, you magnificent Divine Feminine!

- Self-sovereign,

- Self-love and acceptance (*accepting that you might desire to wear beautiful dresses and live in a fancy house, or take luxurious vacations, or to fully embody beauty*),

- Beauty, magnetism, and radiance,

- Deeply intuitive and psychic,

- Channeling (*and also receiving downloads, flowing information from universal consciousness, connecting to the spirit realm, etc.*),

- Balanced in giving/receiving,

- Vulnerable and allowing emotions to flow through,

- Authentic,

- Nurturing and compassionate,

- Healthy boundaries and able to express needs and desires,

- Being present and in the flow,

- Sacred sexuality (*aware of your sexual centers and how to alchemize with them, that you create life and you treat your body with love*), and

- Soul purpose/work (*fulfilling your soul mission and soul desires*)

Section II:

Exercises

Self-Love Practices:

1. Start loving yourself exactly as you are. Go in front of a mirror every day for 21 days minimum, look into your own eyes and say out loud, "I love you exactly as you are!"

   - Notice how your body feels when you say this to yourself. Notice how it gets easier and feels more expansive each day (especially after day 7).

   - This practice strengthens your inner glow (on a soul/energy level).

2. Schedule alone time 3 times per week with only yourself (even if it's for 15-30 minutes). Go do something just for you!

   - For example: yoga outside on the grass/sand, a salt bath (clears energy), hiking, massage, meditation time, etc.

Self-Acceptance Practices:

1. **Body appreciation.** Rub your boobs and tell them you love them and are thankful for them, how beautiful and big or healthy they are, how they provide life and food, etc. <u>Gratitude is key here.</u>

   - Rub different areas for 15-30 seconds each.

   - Feel the love and appreciation for your breasts! (*You can do this for your womb, hands, feet, etc.*)

2. **Celebrate yourself**. Every time something good happens for you, such as you completed a hard work assignment or figured out an issue or planted your entire garden… celebrate it!

    - Hug yourself, jump up and down, create that feeling of excitement of a job well done! You are amazing, so celebrate that!

Section II:

Practice 6:
Clearing Karma

In order to break karmic loops, we need to understand multiple layers of why we repeat cycles. We are here to learn soul lessons, and if we haven't learned and integrated the lesson, we will continue to get tested on it.

This means that the same situation will present itself in different forms until you've 'passed the test'. This can look like: having the same situations arise with a different partner, dating the same kind of wounded guy, inability to sustain weight loss or a healthy body, money not being consistent, your business not flowing or being inconsistent, dissatisfaction in your job or career despite changing locations/workplaces/etc., friendship betrayals or rejections, family dramas, and much more.

We don't want to keep learning the same lessons over and over again. We want to move forward to the next level after we have integrated the soul lessons.

However, in order to do this, we need to look at two specific things: soul contracts/agreements and why we keep looping with the same person, and closing karmic loops by integrating the soul lessons.

First things first.

We will look at Karmic or Soul Contract Clearings so that you are able to detach from the person and clear the soul agreement.

This is especially important if this is a past lover that keeps resurfacing, or a friend who comes in to take advantage of your generosity and then leaves, or a nasty person who just won't go away...

Exercise to "Get off the Wheel of Karma"

One way to break the karmic wheel with a person (from a past relationship, family member, etc.) is to:

1. Close your eyes, and see the person in your mind. Ask your higher self if you have learned all you need to learn from this person and if you soul contract is completed. If the answer is yes, continue the process below.

   If the answer is no, ask what else you need to learn and come back to this once that lesson has been learned and integrated.

2. Envision them in your mind's eye and say to them, "We have completed our soul contract and I let you go from this karmic contract now."

   Ask your higher self to bring forward the contract your souls made with each other, and see yourself tearing that contract up (in your mind).

3. Say out loud, "I let you go with unconditional love. You go your way with love and I'll go mine. And so it is."

Section II:

And you must really mean it, truly feel that you are letting them go with love.

If you still feel resentment, anger, etc. towards them, you have not processed all of the human emotions with them and need to work through that first, forgiving yourself and them. Then come back to this process.

4. Then say out loud, "I forgive myself for anything that I have done to you in this lifetime or any other lifetime, reality or realm. Across all time and space, I forgive myself for any harm that I have done to you or any harm you have done to me in this lifetime or any others. And so it is."

   Then forgive yourself for whatever you did or feel any guilt from (entering into the relationship, judging, fighting, belittling, repeating patterns, etc.).

Another way to clear karma:

For others that you can't remember, or you are simply wishing to clear your energy from everything in the past (karma), you can say this one out loud (you must truly mean it and feel forgiveness):

"I forgive anyone who has harmed me in any way shape or form in this lifetime or in any other lifetimes. I also forgive myself for anything I have done to harm anyone. I clear it and let it go. So it is. Thank you, thank you, thank you!"

Closing Karmic Loops

Integrating Soul Lessons Practice

These karmic cycles and soul lessons look like repeated patterns, traumatic events, dramas, and uncomfortable situations. They tend to be very instrumental in our soul growth and propelling us forward, yet they were usually very painful at the time.

If these lessons have not been completely integrated into your being, you will repeat them continuously. You might even be feeling groggy or slow right now because these energies are asking to be freed from your body and your energetic body.

So here are a few tips to release these past energies in order to make way for the new -> making room for your true soul desires to manifest or be consciously created:

1. **Write down what soul/life lessons you learned in the past 12 months**. For example, what difficult situations arose or what cycles repeatedly arose (such as arguments with family, money issues, or friend betrayals…), and then write down what you learned from these experiences.

   ▶ The soul lesson could be maintaining healthy boundaries, or learning discernment, etc.

2. Sit in a quiet space, take 3 deep belly breaths, and ask your body if the emotions relating to these situations have been completely let go. This can take a few minutes or doing it multiple times, so allow yourself to really feel the emotions and then cleanse with your breath

Section II:

- check into breathwork or somatic sessions if you need more help with clearing emotions.

3. If you still feel connected to the person or situation, this means there is more to clear and an energetic cord/tie to them or the situation still remains. Ask your higher self, guides and spirit team to assist you in removing these cords.

4. Ask your heart if there are any physical items that need to be let go of (in order for the new to come in!), any people who need to be allowed to go from your life, any non-reciprocal or lower aligned relationships, and any limiting beliefs that are stopping you from reaching your desired outcomes.

5. After clearing the past energy and items out of your energetic field and physical space, sit down with a journal and put your hand on your heart. Ask your heart what you're creating this year for your own highest good. You can also ask this to your higher self in meditation for deeper introspection and alignment. (creations in: relationships, money, job/business, home life, trips, etc.)

Repeat any of these practices as you feel called to, or know that something needs to be cleared in your energetic field.

Remember that not everything is ours, so if you feel heavy or that energy must move, ask to send back all energy, beliefs, cords, and thoughts that are not yours to their rightful owner with unconditional love. You should feel relief immediately if it is not yours.

Practice 7:
Subconscious Reprogram

Possibly the most important step (besides trauma work) that we can take for ourselves is reprogramming our subconscious.

We make between 90-95% of our decisions from our subconscious daily, and the subconscious is programmed typically by the age of 7.

Now, the subconscious can carry this current lifetime's wounding as well as a past lifetime's trauma, depending on how much was forgotten when our souls passed through what is called "the veil of amnesia" when we come Gaia side. This is why you might have heard of young children who can remember their most recent past lifetime as a fighter pilot in a war, or living in a country with exotic foods, or how they died, etc. Generally, once they have gone through the school system, they don't remember that lifetime anymore or pushed it away because Western society deems it 'strange' if you remember your past lives.

Yet when we examine our behaviors as an adult, and come to understand that many of our choices stem from our subconscious and that we make those choices without deliberation, then we can start to see where we might need to change some old programming in ourselves.

Section II:

Most of the limiting subconscious programs or beliefs are learned so that we can 'fit in' during school years or in our families, and later on it helps us get 'normal jobs' or attend university.

The reality is that we must choose that we are going to live with our soul guiding the way, not our egos, shadows, subconscious or anything else. We are here to live in our highest alignment with the truth of reality – and the true, organic energetic states for this planet are gratitude, Divine (unconditional) Love, abundance and overflow, happiness and joy, respect and honor, integrity and truth, compassion and empathy along with healthy boundaries and discernment.

These are what some call Fifth Dimensional states of being; energetic vibrations that match a higher consciousness and reality that Lady Gaia, or Gaia, is ascending to. Humanity can either choose this state, or not. *Each soul has its own path, which is to be respected.*

To begin, we will continue to focus on what we desire to bring forth in this lifetime; our soul desires.

Subconscious Reprogramming Exercise

1. Have a journal ready or use your phone. As soon as you wake up/do your morning meditation, write down: "I am happy, grateful, thankful now that…" and write between 1-10 things that your <u>Future Self</u> is thankful for.

    (Examples: My ____ business is a multi-million dollar company, I am a world renown singer, My house is a beautiful, open beach house, My food garden is massive and my kids love it,

My partner relationship is with my wonderful husband, We are happy, loving and laugh a lot..., etc.)

_____

_____

_____

_____

2. Once you've written the 1-10 statements down, sit up with your feet on the ground (either on your bed or in a chair), clear your mind, take a deep breath in, hold it, and say in your head:

   "I am happy, grateful, thankful now that....#1 (the first statement you wrote down)", after you finish saying number 1 in your head, exhale completely.

_____

_____

_____

_____

Section II:

3. Then take another deep breath in, hold it, and say in your head:

   "I am happy, grateful, thankful now that....#2 (the second statement you wrote down)" and exhale your breath.

   _____

   _____

   _____

   _____

   _____

4. And repeat on down your list in the same breathing pattern.

   _____

   _____

   _____

   _____

   _____

   _____

Clearing Blocks

<u>You will need to do this subconscious reprogramming for a minimum of 90 days.</u>

Some people prefer to use affirmations as well, and I highly recommend listening to affirmations before going to sleep and/or upon first waking. This right before sleep/waking time is a great time for the subconscious to be programmed.

If using affirmations spoken by others, please ensure that the script of the affirmations doesn't have negative (no) statements because the brain doesn't understand that i.e. "I am <u>no</u> longer available for…" Look for ones with positive statements only or with a script you can read before you start listening every day.

It is more helpful for your brain to record your voice with the specific affirmations that resonate the most with you at that time and to listen to those on repeat for 15-30 minutes for a minimum of 21 days. Each time you reach a new level, these affirmations will change based on what you are reprogramming in your subconscious.

Section II:

Practice 8:
Energy Reclaim

Keeping our energy and not allowing anyone else to use or siphon it is a huge help in this journey. Sometimes, we don't notice when our energy is being taken or we have given it away consciously or unconsciously.

Sometimes, we have to enforce boundaries and it's not easy because we have never been taught this or we start to give in after a period of time, even if the person has not changed for the positive and cannot be trusted.

Along with reclaiming our energy, there is discernment. Noticing with each and every choice we make, the people who we allow into our lives, the people we text and call, the jobs or businesses we choose, the density or freedom of the location we live – all of it is up to us to discern if it is for us. If it is for our highest alignment and helps assist our energy.

Anything that takes our energy, drains us, or makes us feel small, unworthy or less than – that is not meant for us. We are here to be in our full power, our full energy, and we deserve that!

Which means first we must discern where we can do better at cleaning up our energetic hygiene.

Below are a few tools to assist you in this energy reclamation piece.

Call back your energy:

Every morning before you leave your bed and every night before you sleep, say out loud or in your head:

*"I call my energy back to me now. I call back my energy from anywhere I have consciously or unconsciously given it away or left it behind, across all time and space, in any lifetime, dimension or realm.
I call all of my power back to me now."*

Feel your power coming back to you.

Clearing Cords, Implants and Energetic Attachments:

Equally important is clearing all energetic/ethereal cords, AI implants, and energetic attachments that were placed in your light (energy) body either before birth, once you came Gaia-side (to this planet), during childhood, during your spiritual awakening, etc.

This is a quick meditation to assist you in clearing your bodies. This can help to record in your own voice as a voice note on your phone to do whenever you feel called to, or you feel heavy/sluggish or that something is attached to you.

Section II:

Lying down on your bed or the floor, bring yourself into a meditative state. Focus on your deep belly breaths. Deeply breathing in and out of your nose.

See yourself walking down a hill towards a forest in the sunshine. As you come to the edge of the forest, an ancient massive tree beckons you. As you step towards the tree, you notice there is an old carved door in it, with a golden doorknob. You turn the golden knob and walk through the doorway.

Stepping into the space on the other side, you notice that it is a beautiful, overflowing garden full of flora and fauna. There are little birds flying everywhere and singing happily, the sun is illuminating the space, and this is your sacred healing garden. Perhaps you see a pond or hear a waterfall or fountain. This is your space so whatever you imagine is perfect.

Finding a comfortable spot, you lie down in your healing garden, and you ask your Highest Self and your Spirit Team who are all serving the light only to step forward to assist you today.

Allow them to come forward and feel their energy. Perhaps you will see them in their various forms, or you recognize them. You can feel their unconditional love for you.

Good.

Now ask your team and your higher self to clear all of your bodies from any cords, implants or attachments. See, feel or sense where on your body these are being brought to the light and removed. All cords are severed and sent back to their original owners. All implants are removed and any debris from them as well. The implants are destroyed with the fire of the violet flame. Any attachments are removed now, and sent back to where they came from. You do not consent to any energetic cords, implants or attachments in this lifetime or any other. Across all time and space, you are free from these NOW.

Ask out loud for the golden light of Source to clear all of your bodies and to seal up any holes left from the removals.

Feel the golden light washing over you and pumping throughout your body and blasting out of your heart and into the space around you, into your neighborhood, into your country, and into the whole of Gaia .

Good.

Thank your Spirit Team and your Higher Self for assisting you today. Ask if there's anything else they want you to know today. Wait for their response.

And then see yourself sitting up and standing in your healing garden. Notice if anything has changed in it since when you first came in.

Walk towards the doorway and walk through it, closing the door behind you. As you step back into the meadow at the edge of the forest, look down at your feet. See roots growing from your feet, from your legs, from your root chakra and into the 5D Moth.

Thank her for supporting, loving and nurturing you in this lifetime.

Take a deep breath in and open your eyes.

Section II:

This was energy work so drink plenty of water, rest as you are called to, and allow yourself to feel (and then let go of) whatever emotions come up in the next few days. Be gentle with yourself.

Do this meditation as often as you feel you need to.

Shielding:

One of the easiest ways to protect our energies is to shield them.

In meditation in the morning before you get out of bed, envision a shield of whatever color resonates with you. This shield is strengthened by your higher self and gives you protection against anything that is sent your way by others, and anything that is not in your highest alignment. Ask your guardian angels or your spirit team to assist you in building it if you do not know how. They will show you.

Check on your shield every night before you sleep and clear it by seeing swords cutting any etheric cords that have attached to it, and by sending anything that is not yours back to its owner with unconditional love.

Grief Clearings:

When grief arises, ask it "Whose grief is this?" and/or "Where does this grief come from?" - it will answer you.

Feel it/cry it out and let it go fully from your body.

Then move it lovingly along by saying "I let this grief go completely. I am no longer open to feel grief for this. It is done."

This may need to be done multiple times if this wound is multilayered and deep as there may be lifetimes of grief to let go of in your dna.

Asking for Assistance

(*Energetic and Physical*)

"God Source/Guardians/Angels/Guides, please guide me on my highest aligned path and direct me towards the people that should be in my life for my highest alignment.

I choose my soul, my love, and myself over all others.

I love and trust my inner divine masculine and feminine. Please remove all chaos and lower energies from my life.

Help me be of service to the Divine Plan today, and send me help with_____ (whatever you need assistance with - relationship, money, etc.). I deserve to be fully supported so that I may be of even greater service to my soul purpose and to humanity.

Thank you! Thank you! Thank you!"

Whenever you are feeling down or want some guidance, remember to ask your guides/guardian angels/ancestors for love, support, help and guidance.

They are waiting to help you but you must ask them for exactly what you need (because they can't help unless you ask for it).

Section II:

They will send it to you - sometimes in the form of a chance encounter, butterflies/birds/animals, or a stranger's kindness :)

Section III: Balancing Your Nervous System

Section III:

Nurturing Your Nervous System for

Divine Union

This section is designed to support you on your journey towards expanding your energy, achieving clarity and self-sovereignty, and embracing profound divine connection. The previous work we have done in this workbook might have unsettled your nervous system, or you could already have a strained or frayed nervous system due to the environment you live in and the patriarchal system of the false matrix (*which is currently being replaced with the organic matrix that has both feminine and masculine balance, with more landing in the coming years*).

Most women don't even understand how deeply their nervous system has been impacted because the common theme is to 'just get on with it' until our bodies collapse into panic, anxiety, depression or other diseases from the energy stored inside our bodies that keeps getting piled on top of everything else. I spent many years understanding that my automatic response was "it's fine, everything is fine" and smiling and pretending it was good, while I kept pushing my nervous system to its limit – which resulted in extreme pain and a visit to the psychiatric ward.

Even if you feel that your nervous system is completely regulated, I urge you to read through this section and see the value of a reminder where your system might need some extra love.

In this section, I delve deeper into the practices, supplements, and techniques that I, and my clients, have used.

By incorporating the practices, supplements, and techniques outlined into your daily routine, you will transform and nurture your nervous system, which will assist you on your journey of inner and outer Divine Union.

Understanding the Nervous System

The nervous system is a marvel of intricate connections, functioning as a vital communication network within your body. It consists of two main components: the central nervous system (CNS), which includes the brain and spinal cord, and the peripheral nervous system (PNS), which encompasses the nerves that extend throughout your body.

The nervous system plays a fundamental role in regulating and coordinating various bodily functions, ranging from simple reflexes to complex cognitive processes. It serves as the conduit through which information flows, allowing your body to respond to internal and external stimuli, maintain homeostasis, and support your overall well-being.

When in a state of balance, your nervous system promotes physical, mental, and emotional equilibrium, fostering a sense of harmony within yourself and your surroundings. However, imbalances within the nervous system can hinder your spiritual growth and impede your overall well-being.

Recognizing the signs of a nervous system in need of nurturing is a crucial step on your path to spiritual growth. Here are **some common indicators** that may suggest an imbalance:

- **Chronic Stress and Anxiety**: Excessive stress and anxiety can disrupt the delicate balance of your nervous system. Persistent feelings of tension, restlessness, or an inability to relax may be signals that your nervous system requires support.

- **Fatigue and Sleep Disturbances**: A fatigued nervous system can manifest as chronic fatigue, difficulty sleeping, or disrupted sleep patterns. If you often feel tired despite adequate rest or struggle with insomnia, it may be an indication that your nervous system needs nurturing.

- **Mood Swings and Emotional Instability**: The nervous system influences your emotional well-being. Imbalances can lead to mood swings, irritability, emotional sensitivity, and difficulty managing stress. These emotional fluctuations may suggest an underlying need for nervous system support.

- **Poor Concentration and Cognitive Function**: Your nervous system plays a vital role in cognitive processes, including attention, memory, and focus. If you experience difficulties with concentration, memory recall, or cognitive function, it may be a sign that your nervous system could benefit from nurturing.

- **Physical Symptoms**: Imbalances in the nervous system can manifest as physical symptoms such as headaches, muscle tension, digestive issues, or a weakened immune system. These symptoms can serve as valuable cues to pay attention to your nervous system's well-being.

- **Consistent Psychic Attacks or Feeling Attacked in the Spirit Realm:** If you feel you are being psychically attacked or attacked during dream time, which can result in headaches, physical ailments and more, it is especially important to make sure that you are paying attention to your nervous system and allowing yourself rest time as well as time and space from others. *Also, the more trauma and shadow work you do, the less you should feel anyone being able to attack you on any level.*

By recognizing these signs and understanding the importance of nurturing your nervous system, you can take proactive steps to restore balance and support your spiritual growth.

Remember, your nervous system is a gateway to higher states of consciousness and profound connection. By gaining a deeper understanding of its intricate workings and recognizing the signs of imbalance, you are taking a significant stride.

Section III:

Supplements and Nutrients

As with anything, do your research and check in with your intuition/ higher self or holistic doctor.

1. **My favorite green mix - Green Vibrance.** It is a mixture of vitamins, nutrients and herbs delivering everything from liver cleansing to probiotics (gut health!!!) to energy.

2. **Adaptogenic Herbs:** Adaptogens are a class of herbs that help the body adapt to stress and promote balance. They support the nervous system by modulating the body's stress response and promoting a sense of calm. Some popular adaptogens include Ashwagandha, Rhodiola Rosea, Holy Basil, and Ginseng. These herbs can help reduce anxiety, improve mood, and enhance overall well-being.

3. **Omega-3 Fatty Acids:** Omega-3 fatty acids, particularly EPA (eicosapentaenoic acid) and DHA (docosahexaenoic acid), are essential fats that play a crucial role in brain health and cognitive function. They are known to support the nervous system by reducing inflammation, improving neurotransmitter function, and promoting overall mental well-being. Sources of omega-3 fatty acids include fatty fish (such as salmon and mackerel), chia seeds, flaxseeds, and walnuts.

4. **B Vitamins:** B vitamins, including B6, B12, and folate (B9), are essential for nervous system health. They support the production of neurotransmitters, such as serotonin and dopamine, which regulate mood and cognitive function. B vitamins also aid in the formation of myelin, a protective

covering around nerve fibers. Dietary Sources of B vitamins include leafy greens, legumes, whole grains, eggs, and lean meats.

5. **Magnesium:** Magnesium is a vital mineral that plays a crucial role in nerve function and relaxation. It helps regulate neurotransmitters, supports muscle relaxation, and promotes a sense of calm. Magnesium-rich foods include dark leafy greens, nuts, seeds, and whole grains. Magnesium supplements, such as magnesium citrate or magnesium glycinate, can also be beneficial, particularly for individuals with low magnesium levels or increased stress.

6. **Turmeric and others:** Turmeric is great for your joints if you feel aches or have joint issues (which can affect your nerves).

   a. Reishi mushrooms are great for calming/sleeping, cold sores, and boosting your immune system, but I highly recommend a mushroom blend if you want mental clarity, calm, brain health and more!

   b. Organic CBD capsules or gummies are amazing if you experience the feeling of being unable to ground your energy, which can happen during specific energy shifts and spikes throughout the year.

   c. Valerian Root drops (or tea) will help to stabilize your nervous system, especially if you feel anxious, stressed or are heading into a holiday season or high stress period. Take as many drops as you need!

Section III:

   d. Organic Blue Lotus flowers (used in tea) for assisting with sleep are amazing as well as can also assist with lucid dreaming and a deeper connection with your higher self and spirit guides! Add a spoonful of honey so it is not as bitter and test using 1 flower for your first time preparing the tea, then you can increase it. (*There are many sellers of organic blue lotus flowers on etsy.*)

   e. A balanced diet full of fruits, veggies, lean proteins, and ph balanced, purified water is really beneficial to our bodies and systems as well. Consider it a part of your own self-love to eat fresh (local if possible) and well. Intuitive eating will assist you as well because every body is different and requires different things at different cycles throughout the year.

It's important to note that while the supplements and nutrients I've mentioned can support the nervous system, it's always advisable to *consult with your healthcare professional or qualified nutritionist* before starting any new supplements or making significant dietary changes.

Understand that if the body has parasites, a build up of heavy metals and other issues, the nutrients and supplements will not make any difference. The body should be cleansed first. The majority of people on this planet (especially if they are from the USA) will need to detox quite often.

Detoxing or Cleanses

I, as well as most of my clients and friends, do fasting, detoxing and cleanses as well. Typically, these are done in accordance with your higher self guidance (*versus ego, "everyone is doing it!"*) and should be done under supervision of a qualified professional if you have never done these before.

This can look differently for everyone, and it is important that you are nutritionally stable for these types of physical body purifiers. Please seek a nutritionist or holistic doctor to tell you more about this and get a report on your body..

I use a heavy metal detox drop regimen first, to clear any brain fog and densities. This is followed by a 2 week parasite cleanse (drops) with charcoal capsules to bind the parasites and L-Ornithine to get rid of the ammonia that dying parasites secrete in our bodies. Parasites tend to hide behind heavy metals, so it's important to do the heavy metal detox first.

Following these cleanses, a 3-4 day water or herbal tea fast (no food, caffeine, etc.), or a juice fast, is recommended. The cells start to regenerate after the 72 hour mark.

The cleanses and fasts all assist with anti-aging, spiritual communication/higher connection and consciousness, and healing the body. This healing of the body will in turn assist in the re-stabilization of the nervous system (but should not be undertaken if you suffer from extreme anxiety and depression).

When fasting or doing a parasite cleanse, try to do it around a full moon as this will assist you in clearing even more. *Please research this for yourself.*

There are colon cleanses and colonics, kidney cleanses, liver cleanses and more. These are all important for the body, especially if you have never done one or were raised in a household where healthy food, detoxing and vitamins/herbs were <u>not</u> regimented. The goal of all of these cleanses and detoxes is to assist the body (the vessel) in its absorption of vitamins and minerals, as well as to function properly for the length of time your soul requires you to inhabit the body you are in.

<u>Again, all of this should be researched by your own self and a trusted qualified professional should be taken on board to assist.</u>

Breathwork Techniques:

Breathwork techniques are powerful tools that tap into the innate wisdom of your body and activate the body's relaxation response. By consciously working with your breath, you can move stagnant energy, calm and reset the nervous system, and cultivate a harmonious state within yourself. Below are some techniques to explore and integrate into your life.

- **Deep Belly Breathing:** Also known as diaphragmatic breathing or belly breathing, this technique involves consciously breathing deeply into your belly. By expanding your diaphragm and filling your lungs with oxygen-rich air, you activate the body's relaxation response, reduce stress, and promote a sense of calm.

- Sitting in a comfortable position, place one hand on your belly and exhale all of the air out of your mouth. Feel your belly contract and empty of air. Breathe deeply into your nose for 5 seconds and fill your belly up with air, feeling it expand outwards. Exhale the breath out of your belly through your nose for 5 seconds. Then repeat for 3-5 minutes.

- **Alternate Nostril Breathing:** This pranayama technique involves alternating the breath through the nostrils, balancing the flow of energy in the body. It helps harmonize the nervous system, quiet the mind, and enhance overall well-being.

    - Sit up straight (lotus position or on a chair with feet touching the ground), hold your right nostril shut with your middle and fourth finger of your right hand, breathe in through the unblocked nostril into the back of your throat and into your belly. Now place those same fingers on the left nostril, and then exhale the air out of the right nostril. Breathe into the right nostril, then place your fingers onto the right nostril, and exhale out of the left nostril. Repeat this for 2-5 minutes.

- **Breath Retention Practices:** These techniques involve intentionally holding the breath for specific durations. For example, you might practice inhaling for 3 seconds, retaining the breath for 3 seconds, and exhaling for 3 seconds, and then retaining no breath for 3 seconds - in a controlled manner. Breath retention practices, when done safely and under guidance, can help build resilience, increase energy flow, and deepen your connection with your body. You can increase the length of time you hold and exhale as you practice.

- Check out breathwork for beginners on Insight Timer if you require assistance, or attend a class. There is a lot of resistance to doing breathwork as most people 'think' they don't need it. *I promise you, it is life changing and I do it 2-3 times per week.*

  - On Insight Timer, check out Kirsty Lyon's guided breathwork sessions.

Yoga

Yoga, an ancient Vedic practice that unites mind, body, and spirit, offers a myriad of benefits for nurturing and regulating the nervous system. Some yoga, such as Yin Yoga, focuses on the fascia which assists our entire body, as well as the nervous system.

Below are some yoga poses, videos, and meditation techniques to support your journey towards nervous system harmony and Divine Union.

Asanas (Yoga Poses): There are two yoga poses that remain the most beneficial - especially if you are new to yoga - to remember. *Cat/Cow is also great for your spine staying limber and moving energy.*

- Child's Pose (Balasana): this is complete surrender. Holding this pose (the regular or extended version) is the most freeing and emotional releasing pose for those times we need to surrender to the Divine and relax into just simply being. *Do not force yourself to sit your behind on your feet! Allow your body to settle into its natural state and eventually know that you will be able to rest your behind on your feet with practice.*

Regular Child's Pose (knees together, feet touching):

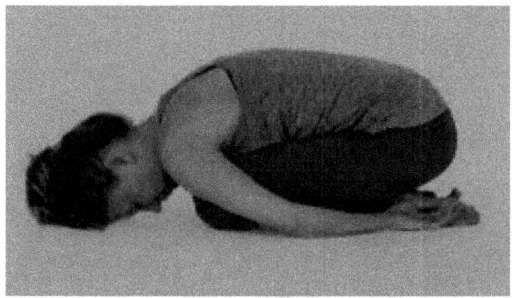

(image from ekhartyoga.com)

Extended Child's Pose (knees open wide, big toes touching):

(image from freestock.com)

- Legs-up-the-wall Pose (Viparita Karani): this pose really can help you sleep if you struggle with falling asleep or getting back to sleep. You can do it against a wall or with your legs straight up in the air. Either way, you're reversing the blood flow and it's an amazing relaxation technique.

Section III:

Legs Up The Wall Pose (press your behind up against the wall, keep your knees slightly bent until you can extend them fully - takes practice!!!)

(image from worldpeaceyogaschool.com)

Yoga Video: Finding a beginner yin yoga video they resonate with is what I recommend to my clients. Yin yoga is the feminine balancing yoga, and is a great tool for regulating our nervous system in a world of constant go-go-going!

Other yoga practices I love to incorporate include Hatha (more gentle) and Vinyasa (if you feel that you are too in your feminine energy and are not taking enough action!). Any type of restorative yoga is going to help your nervous system and body.

Pranayama (Breath Control): Pranayama exercises involve conscious control and regulation of the breath. Specific pranayama techniques, such as Nadi Shodhana (Alternate Nostril Breathing) and Ujjayi Breathing (Victorious Breath), help regulate the nervous system, enhance breath awareness, and deepen your connection to the present moment. (*There are plenty of free videos on Youtube if you feel called to go deeper into these practices. As always, find a practitioner online or in person who you resonate with.*)

Meditation Techniques: Not everyone can sit in stillness and meditate. I highly recommend doing meditation after you do yoga, breathwork, go for a walk, or some other energy clearing exercise. Use Insight Timer if you prefer to listen to someone guide you (especially if you're just beginning to learn meditation).

By incorporating these nutritional, breathwork and yoga practices into your daily routine, you can create a sacred space for nurturing your nervous system, releasing tension and repressed emotions, and deepening your connection to the Divine.

As we know that the inner is physically reflected in the outer reality, your body and your system are as important as the energetic work that you do. If you are embodied in true health and wealth, it is literally seen in your appearance - the glow from within and the health of the body.

Any imbalance, dis-ease, illness, etc. showcases the need for more inner work and releasing something that is being stored in the body and energetic centers.

There are many other ways to help your nervous system including EFT, EMDR, Pilates, Qi Gong, Somatic exercises, dance, taking naps, and more. You can also search for meditations or exercises that reset the Vagus Nerve.

Find what works for you and your nervous system and keep nurturing it!

Part 2

Section IV:
Activating Your Soul Purpose and Gifts

Another part of coming into our inner Divine Union is claiming our soul gifts and soul purpose. This goes hand-in-hand with HIM appearing in your life, if you are looking for your physical Counterpart.

If you have not claimed who you truly are, or disregard your soul's guidance, or deny your inherent spiritual gifts that you earned over lifetimes - how can he SEE you? If he is truly the Divine Masculine incarnate (a King, a Leader, etc.), then he will expect you to be fully expressing yourself as well. You stepping fully into your purpose and gifts lights you up from the inside out. If you are dimming your light, he can't magnetize towards you.

The work in the previous sections is about stepping more fully into your truth, into your self-sovereignty and allowing yourself to be who you came here to be. To live in the way you came here to live. To be free, happy, abundant, grateful, expansive, connected to the Divine... -> all of it!

This is the lifetime for you to fulfill your life path - the path you plotted out before you incarnated. The one you completely forgot when you were born or as a child.

The path that you are remembering NOW.

Let's start with psychic/spiritual abilities or gifts.

We know that everyone on this planet has psychic abilities (that have become blocked, forgotten or unused over time).

Your spiritual gifts are varied and can be very useful in this lifetime. You are the only one who can understand which gifts you have and how to use them for the highest good. *Nobody else has any*

Section IV:

command over your gifts or abilities, unless you give your power away to them, or have made a contract/agreement with them.

These are the <u>4 main psychic gifts</u> on this planet:

- Clairvoyance - the ability to see beyond what is visible.

- Clairaudience - the ability to hear. What do we hear? Our angels, our guides, our higher selves.

- Claircognizance - the ability to think clearly and achieve a deep sense of knowing. Info dropping into your head/crown chakra.

- Clairsentience - the ability to feel and perceive (gut instinct).

I will add a few more here:

- Ability to see people's/animals/trees/ beings auras.

- Clairempathy - to feel others emotions or spirit's emotions.

- Clairtangency - This is also known as Psychometry. You are able to receive a message by touching or holding an object in your hands.

Most of us lead with one or two of the 'claire's' listed above, but we are all born with them. We can enhance them and unlock greater abilities with them the more we focus on them.

Getting these working easily takes practice, discipline and consistency. The more you exercise them, the faster or easier you will experience them or use them.

Here are two questions to ask yourself:

I. Which are you most drawn to or want to work on? \

_____

_____

II. Which do you feel that you already have control over?

_____

_____

There are more that you can investigate on your own, but starting with those "claire's" gives you a starting point. Notice which ones you are drawn to or pop out to you the most (interest you or your spirit jumps at).

Exercise to Increase Abilities:

- Choose the 'claire' that you have the most control over.

- Meditate on that gift. Ask your guides if it's the first one for you to pursue.

- <u>If it is the one you should start with, commit to 1 month of meditating on this ability every day for 5-10 minutes to begin with.</u> This time will increase as you get better.

- Usually when you work with 1, others start to flow (opening the floodgates).

- After 1-2 months of consistency, move into exploring the other ones that call to you or that your guides have nudged you towards.

Daily Mantra:

(Say out loud every day for 21+ days)

*"I am strengthening and honing my psychic gifts.
I expand with more wisdom from my higher self daily.
I am in touch with my divinity.
My powers grow daily as I receive guidance for the highest good of all.*

(anything else you want to add)

Thank you! Thank you! Thank you!"

Psychic Power Honing

As with anything we want to be good at, practice helps to strengthen the muscle.

1. Meditate as called or at minimum 5-10 minutes 4-5 times per week on using your gifts.

2. Create an energetic cleansing method for before and after you meditate to ask the questions below. Maybe it's a prayer of protection to your guides and burning sage or a white candle before and after. It's important to protect your energy when you view or travel in other dimensions.

3. Ask specific questions to your higher self. For example:

   a. "I want to see behind the veil. Please show me (a specific planet, people, dead ancestor, specific lifetime, etc.)..." - this will hone your ability by focusing on a specific location or person. *Practice practice practice!*

   b. "I want to see... (my soul family, my galactic family, the planet I came from before this one) - whatever you want to see. As you practice this on yourself, eventually, you will be able to do this for other people (potential clients/people you help) as well.

   c. Telepathy - practice with an animal or child first. Send them a message in your head. Something simple like sending a picture of food (a snack, a cookie, etc.) or if they want to play (use a favorite toy as the picture you send mentally). See how they respond.

Sometimes, as we are practicing our gifts and because most people don't understand their own spiritual abilities, we can feel as if we are unsure or like an imposter. Imposter syndrome is real and it is something to be aware of.

However, if you are constantly integrating your ego and shadows, and consistently communicating with your higher self, your spirit guides and team and Source, then you are unable to be an imposter. It shows integrity and humbleness that you have the ability to question yourself and everything.

We came here with a specific mission(s) and we understand, on a soul level, that we will do what we came here to do in this lifetime.

Section IV:

And that means that we are allowing ourselves to claim ALL of our gifts, to hone them, and to eventually be able to use them (almost) effortlessly.

Ask your spirit team all of the questions. Ask Source why something is the way it is. Ask your higher self what the heck is happening and what you need to know that day. **Be like a child in your wonder of the universe and your own gifts**. Ask all of the questions and receive the answers, even if it takes a few days to get them.

You deserve all of the love and fun – and using your gifts is not just about work or service. They are also for you to have fun with, to ask the questions, to assist your own self as well!

Connecting with Your Guides

(You know in your soul that you are protected from higher realms and you know that you have guides.)

Sit in a quiet place where you won't be disturbed Write down the questions you have in your journal. Get into a meditative state and set the intention to meet your spirit guides, spirit team and/or ancestors who are serving the light only.

Ask for any clarity around them (i.e. who they are, names, where they're from, how long they've been with you, etc.). This can help us to speed up our soul path or can open new dimensions.

If you are having a rough day or need clarity on an issue, ask them to help you.

Meditate when you are feeling calm and relaxed and because you want to, not because you feel you have to. This should be a fun exercise and building up the relationships with your guides can only assist your journey on this planet.

Continue this practice until you feel comfortable with communicating and learning from them.

Soul Purpose Prayer:

"I open my heart to my soul purpose.

God, please guide me on my path and direct me towards the people that should be in my life. Protect my energy and show me anything I need to see in a way I will understand.

I choose my soul and myself over all others.
I love and trust the divine masculine and feminine.

Please remove all chaos and lower energies from my life.

Thank you, thank you, thank you!
I am FREE, I am HERE, and I am LOVE!"

Notice any reactions you have in your body (tingling, warmth, etc.).

Section IV:

Soul Purpose Activation

Integral to inner union is <u>knowing</u> your purpose. Why you're here at this time. What you're doing and the steps to take to fulfill that purpose/mission.

This purpose can be based upon cycles of 3-9 years, which is dependent upon your soul, and can change once a mission or a soul level is completed. *However, there can be one specific mission that you are here to achieve throughout this lifetime that can take on various forms as you evolve and complete soul lessons.*

If you are still wondering what you are here to do, here is a meditation to record in your own voice in order to activate your soul purpose. *If you already know why you're here, skip to the next meditation.*

Record yourself on your phone so that you can listen to this in a relaxed meditative state. <u>*Have a journal ready to write down all of the answers you receive during this meditation.*</u>

Lying down on your back, breathing in and out, releasing all that no longer serves as you exhale. Breathing deeply into the belly, expanding it with love and light. Keep focusing on your breath as you breathe in and out of your nose. Allow yourself to sink deeper and deeper into the ground, into your body, and into Gaia with each inhale.

As you focus on your body and each breath, notice where your body feels tight or there is tension. Send your breath to that area and clear the energy there with each exhale.

Say out loud: "This space is holy, this space is protected, this space is clear. I only consent to assistance from my highest self at this time."

In your head, ask your highest self to step forward in whatever way she wants to show up today to assist you on this soul purpose activation. Notice how you feel when she arrives.

How does her energy feel….What does she look like?

Sense or see her smiling at you with unconditional love.

Ask her to clear your body with the golden light of Source before you begin. Feel the golden light spreading throughout every cell in your body, through every bone and muscle and tendon, through your fascia, through every energy center, and through every hair on your head.

Good.

Now ask her to pull up your soul purpose at this time. What is it?

This can be a word, a sense, a picture, or a feeling. It can be a scene from a movie or a description. There is no judgment.

Ask her for more clarity about your soul purpose if you need it.

Take a few moments here and keep asking her questions until you completely understand what it is you are here to do at this time. Write down whatever she says.

Good.

Section IV:

Close your eyes again and relax back into this meeting with your highest self.

Ask her to help you integrate your soul purpose completely at this time. Notice where she directs her energy to in your body. This can be to your heart, your sacral or your solar plexus chakra.

Good.

State out loud: "My soul purpose is completely activated and integrated now. I remain rooted and committed to my purpose and know that I am completely protected, guided and supported by Source at all times. Thank you, thank you, thank you!"

Next, ask your highest self to clear your channel to open up to more nudges from Source and your Spirit Team and her for your next steps to fulfill your soul purpose.

Feel the golden light of Source streaming through your crown chakra and flowing through your entire system, opening up your channel to your purpose completely.

Ask her if there is anything else that needs to happen today for total integration. *Pause here as needed.*

Ask her if there is any action step you need to take today towards your soul purpose. Write down whatever she says.

Ask her to bring forward any Spirit Guide or team member who is serving the light only and is here to specifically help you fulfill your soul purpose on Gaia at this time.

Wait to see, sense or feel what being steps forward. Who is this being? What do they look or feel like? What words are coming to you? Do you remember them from any other lifetimes or missions?

Now ask them the following questions and write down their answers in your journal:

- What are they here to help you with?

- What are you supposed to call them?

- How do they want you to interact with them?

- What do they want you to know or do today?

- How many lifetimes have they worked with you?

Good.

Thank them for showing up today and for being here to assist you! Tell them you will see them soon.

And then thank your highest self for all of her help today! Thank her for being there for you always and that you will check in with her again soon.

Thank you to all of your spirit team, spirit guides, ancestors, and everyone assisting you who serve the light only. Thank you Source for your unconditional love and presence.

Now look down at your feet and imagine tree roots growing out of your feet, out of your root chakra, out of your legs into Lady Gaia, into the core of the Great Mother. Thank her for her support, her love

Section IV:

and her guidance on this earthly journey. Take a deep breath in and open your eyes.

Take a few minutes to journal about this experience and see what else comes through for you.

Soul Purpose Deepening:

During meditation, asking your Inner Divine Feminine:

- "What is the next level of my work?"

- "What do I need to do to expand into my next level of my soul purpose work and service to humanity?"

Write down whatever she tells you so that you can refer back to it. Listening to her and implementing what she says will magnify your capacity to receive more.

After you have written down everything that she says, ask your Spirit Team and Spirit Guides to help you fulfill those action items. *They are here to help you and your inner masculine stay on your soul purpose path and to clear the way energetically for your magic and alignment to opportunities and abundance/overflow to occur with ease and flow.*

Write down anything they tell you to take action steps on as well. Refer back to it consistently until everything from your Inner Feminine and Spirit Teams have asked you to do is completed.

Repeat this exercise after you've completed the tasks. <u>Each new level requires new actions for your expansion and growth!</u>

A side note here: *If you are seeking to attract your physical Divine Counterpart, committing to and continuously doing your soul purpose work lights you up; it is a big part of being in Inner Divine Union.*

When HE sees you doing what you love and all lit up, this magnetizes him to you and it also brings him immense joy and pleasure. HE loves to see you inspired, radiant and creating your passions!

Section V:
Aligning to your Inner Union

"Because Divine Union is the most powerful creation energy. When two humans, beings, creators, meld their energy into sacred unification connected to the Divine, they cannot be separated or stopped. They are the stories of legends. They are unshakable and determined to create for the highest good of all. They are creating lasting positive change on this planet. The Divine Unions are building heavenly kingdoms with Gaia based in Divine Love, respect, honor and integrity.
As within, so without." - Acacia Lawson

Connecting more to your inner aspects is a beautiful journey of expansion. Eventually, the sacred union between the inner feminine and masculine is harmonious, supportive, loving and respectful.

In order to get there, we will look at how you are currently seeing them and communicating with these internal aspects.

But first, do you know what a healthy inner feminine energy is and a healthy inner masculine energy feels like?

For example, the healthy masculine delegates to others in order to not waste his own energy. For example, if he's not good at marketing, he pays for it to be done (within a certain budget and timeframe - structure!). He knows he does not have to do or be great at everything and that everyone has different zones of genius. He takes inspired actions based on the true soul desires of his Queen, his inner feminine.

The healthy feminine rests and doesn't *DO* all the time. How many things do you "have to do" in a day? Do you give your body and mind

Section V:

time to simply sit and do nothing? To be absolutely still (besides breathing)? If you made a list of everything you do in 1 day (besides cooking or taking care of your kids - which is necessary), are there more than 10 things on that list? Are you in constant overdrive? Are you giving your feminine aspect the love, rest and attention she deserves?

The more we build our relationship up with these inner aspects of ourselves, the more they can assist us and help us expand even more into our true state - Divine Love.

Firstly, we will do a meditation to meet these inner aspects. Secondly, you can work on building up your relationships with them by doing the Communication Exercises located after the meditations.

Meditations

Please record your voice saying these meditations to yourself. They will be more powerful.

Inner Masculine:

Sitting in a comfortable position with back straight and taking 3 big, deep, belly breaths in through the now. Exhaling out through the mouth and sighing it all out. Again, breathing deeply into the belly. And exhaling all that no longer serves with a big sigh. And one last time, inhaling in through the nose and sighing it all out the mouth.

Now breathe in and out of the nose, in and out of the belly. Relaxing the mind and the nervous system. There is nowhere to be and nothing to do. Keep breathing in and out, slowly and gently now.

Good.

Focus on the third eye, bringing all awareness and energy there. Breathe into the third eye. Feel the energy flowing there. Focusing on the breath.

Now as you relax even deeper, see, sense or feel a long hallway with a golden light at the end. Walk down that hallway and towards the golden pulsating light.

With each step, you feel your energy relaxing and you feel something amazing is going to happen.

That golden light turns out to be a golden doorway, and as you pause in front of the doorway, you see that this big door is carved full of wonderful symbols and shapes. Whatever comes into your mind is what you need to see, sense or feel here. There is no judgment.

You reach out your hand and turn the golden doorknob on the door and open the door. As you step through the doorway, you notice that you are now in your own sacred healing space. This is your unique space, suited to your multidimensional healing. Looking around you, you might see large trees and plants, a fountain or pond, or a healing room that is comfortable and luxurious. Anything you sense or see is the right thing for you at this time. This is your healing space.

Wonderful.

Now call forward your inner Divine Masculine. Ask him to show up however he wants to show up today.

Section V:

And see how he comes forward to you. How does he show up? What does he look like? What does his energy feel like? How does he walk or move?

Is he angry or sad? Does he feel neglected or looked over? Does he feel that he's not listened to or disregarded or disrespected?

What is he telling or showing you? What do you sense here?

Good.

Now ask him a question in your head. He can respond to you telepathically or you might sense or feel his response.

My Inner Masculine, what's my relationship with you like?

Listen to his response. Acknowledge his answer and respond however you feel called.

Good. Ask some more questions and pause after each question to wait for his responses.

Are you in any pain? *(pause)*

How are you showing up in my relationship with men? *(pause)*

How are you showing up in my relationship with women? *(pause)*

How are you affecting my money or my business/career? *(pause)*

Are you happy and feeling loved? *(pause)*

How can I listen to you more or get to know you better? *(pause)*

Good. Take as much time with him as you would like in this space.

Once you are ready to leave, tell him you will come back very soon and visit with him again and that you love him and are so happy he is here with you, always!

Does he smile at you and agree? What is his reaction to your words?

Then take a look around your healing space. See if anything has changed. And then walk towards the door and pull it open. Step out and back into the hallway and walk back down it. Back towards the darkness of the universal space.

And then stop and look down at your feet. See tree roots growing out of your feet, out of your root chakra, and into Gaia. Into the core of the Great Mother. We thank Lady Gaia for her love, her support and her guidance on this journey.

Take a deep breath in and open your eyes.

(end of meditation)

So that is your inner masculine!

Get to know HIM. Use the exercises further down in this section to build up your relationship with him even more.

The stronger your relationship with him, the more everything outside of you starts to shift and expand.

Section V:

Inner Feminine:

Sitting in a comfortable position with your back straight and taking 3 big, deep, belly breaths in through the nose. Exhaling out through your mouth and sighing it all out loudly if you need to. Again, breathing in deeply into the belly, and exhaling all that no longer serves out of you with a big sigh. And one last time, inhaling in through the nose and sighing it all out the mouth.

Now breathe in and out of the nose, in and out of the belly. Relaxing the mind and the nervous system. There is nowhere to be and nothing to do. Keep breathing in and out, slowly and gently.

Good.

Focus on the third eye, bringing all awareness and energy there. Breathe into the third eye. Feel the energy flowing there. Focusing on the breath.

As you relax even deeper, see, sense or feel a long hallway with a golden light at the end. Walk down that hallway and towards the golden pulsating light.

With each step, you feel your energy relaxing and you feel something amazing is going to happen.

That golden light turns out to be a golden doorway, and as you pause in front of the doorway, you see that this big door is carved full of wonderful symbols and shapes. Whatever comes into your mind is what you need to see, sense or feel here. There is no judgment.

You reach out your hand and turn the golden doorknob on the door and open the door. As you step through the doorway, you notice that you are now in your own sacred healing space. This is your unique space, suited to your multidimensional healing. Looking around you, you might see large trees and plants, a fountain or pond, or a healing room that is comfortable and luxurious. Anything you sense or see is the right thing for you at this time. This is your healing space.

Notice if anything has changed in your sacred healing space? Is the energy clearer? More water or plants or trees? Or is it the same?

Is anyone else joining you here today in this space like your higher self or a spirit guide who is serving the light only?

Good.

Now call forward your inner Divine Feminine. Ask Her to show up however she wants to show up today.

And see how she comes forward to you. How does she show up? What does she look like? What's her energy feel like? How does she walk or move?

Is she angry or sad? Does she feel neglected or looked over? Does she feel that she's not listened to or is disregarded or disrespected?

What is she telling or showing you? What do you sense here with her? *(pause)*

Good.

Now ask her a question in your head. She can respond to you telepathically or you might sense or feel his response.

My Inner Feminine, what's my relationship with you like?

Section V:

Listen to her response. Acknowledge her answer and respond however you feel called.

Good. Ask some more questions and pause after each question to wait for his responses.

Are you in any pain? *(pause)*

How are you showing up in my relationship with women? *(pause)*

How are you showing up in my relationship with men? *(pause)*

How are you showing up in my money or my business/career? Or how are you affecting it? *(pause)*

Are you happy and feeling loved? *(pause)*

How can I listen to you more or get to know you better? *(pause)*

Good. Take as much time with her as you would like in this space.

Once you are ready to leave, tell her that you will come back very soon and visit with her again and that you love her and are so happy that she is here with you, always!

Does she smile at you and agree? What is her reaction to your words?

Wonderful.

Then take a look around your healing space. See if anything has changed. And then walk towards the door and pull it open. Step out and back into the hallway and walk back down it. Back towards the darkness of the universal space.

And then stop and look down at your feet. See tree roots growing out of your feet, out of your root chakra, and into Gaia. Into the core of the Great Mother. We thank Lady Gaia for her love, her support and her guidance on this journey.

Take a deep breath in and open your eyes.

(end of meditation)

And that is your inner feminine!

Get to know HER. Use the exercises below to build up your relationship with her even more.

The stronger your relationship with her, the more ideas you will receive and the more you will be open to receive all that is yours by your Divine birthright.

Communication Exercises

Inner Masculine:

Write a letter to your inner Divine Masculine (*he's your action taker, provider, has the quickest/easiest/best route for you to take*) - feel into him and ask him questions/create a dialogue,

Section V:

- Questions to ask: "Why have you felt rejected or neglected by me", "Why did he feel he needed to abandon you, Why doesn't he trust you?"

- Have a dialogue with him, ask him how he truly feels. What is his answer?

- Ask yourself: "Why don't I trust my inner masculine?" "Do I always have one foot out the door, ready to run?"

- With your heart, ask him: "What is it that you need from me, my inner masculine?"

- Speak into those hidden areas - your inner feminine needs to see and love the hidden parts as well

Example response: Your Inner Divine Masculine says, "I don't trust that you will honor yourself and speak up for yourself, that you will lose yourself in a new relationship/job/ business/friendship again, repeating the same lessons or becoming codependent again; that we will lose our sovereignty and you will lose everything we have created in this life/business again, we will lose our freedom and we will be in codependency and enmeshment and losing of our true self and mission/purpose"

Example response: You respond with, "I've pushed you away and I apologize. I've sabotaged this thing that I really desire - (i.e. a marriage, children, relationship, business, career) - I feel that you are catastrophizing it already. How can I understand what you need from me and how we can work together for my highest good?"

- - Can you make space to hear him and understand him and invite him back in, and love him? Allow him to speak to you and allow yourself to speak back.

    a. Another letter to him: How can I be of service to you, my masculine, my warrior king? How can I love you more or show you that I will never lose myself or my mission/purpose when I'm in a relationship?

    b. Think of him as a lover: write him a love letter praising all of the things you love about him and how grateful you are for all he does for you (the great job/business you have now, great fun, the money coming in, the new house, the new location etc)

Inner Feminine:

Write a letter to your inner Divine Feminine (*she's your intuition, your soul, your nurturer that has the wisdom for your divine masculine to take action from*)

- "How can I honor you better, how can you trust me, how can you feel my love, how have I let you down, how have I not trusted you, my Divine Feminine?" etc.

- Feel into it. Create the dialogue and keep it going until you have come to a conclusion that you both want the same thing (loving relationship, different job, money/new business, etc. and will trust, listen to and love each other to get there)

Section V:

Continue practicing the letters or meditating and asking questions to them for a minimum of 21 days. This solidifies it as a habit and ensures you will stay committed to both of these aspects and their wellbeing.

As you continue building up a relationship with your inner Divine Feminine and Masculine, you will sense internally that they are both there (some days one is more prevalent than the other depending on what is needing to be done in your life).

They are always loving and always have your back – they want you to have everything you truly desire from your soul!

If any responses during these exercises are super negative or mean, take the time to ask where they truly came from - if they came from your ego/pain body/angry 6 year old self, etc.

Ask your higher self how you can heal that part of yourself from any fears or negativity that are at the root of any negative/mean answers that have come up.

Section VI:
Consciously Creating Your Divine Inner Union

Section VI:

There are various stages of this inner union journey, and if any of the processing, releasing, integration and activations from the previous foundational work in this workbook have not taken place, the inner union has not been committed to fully. I highly recommend going back to look at the sections on past life wounding, shadow work and any subconscious reprogramming that might need to take place.

When you have completed and processed the exercises and processes in this book, you will feel a massive shift. Each of these exercises generally takes a 21 day minimum of consistent dedication to energetically shift. It can take another 20-60 days from that 21st day to see external changes in our physical reality due to residual energy. If you have noticed on day 61 that there has been no shift (and you are still doing the exercises), please go back and do them again. Sometimes, the ego/pain body has more control than is realized and it can take longer for these new ways of BEing to sink in.

Every exercise in this book is about the foundational work of inner union so that you can never be shaken from it. This is what we consider mastering the inner union and embodying it - by doing these "basics" (exercises) and remembering to go back to them when you feel wobbly or out of alignment, you are mastering Inner Divine Union.

I still do these exercises and have built upon them, as each new level requires another version of deepening into union.

All of this work can be facilitated more quickly by working with someone aligned to your highest timeline and who is living in a physical Divine Union. Ask your higher self if you have a soul contract with the person to work on your Inner Divine Union initiation and activation.

And congratulations if you have seen and felt massive shifts and changes in your inner and outer worlds! That the masculine (men, structure/provision, and money!) is showing up much more for you, lovingly and consistently, in a healthy way. That the women who surround you are supportive and nurturing with healthy boundaries, and that your creative ideas are flowing with ease and joy. That your inner child feels happy and jubilant because she gets to play and have fun with you.

(These areas should be in alignment for 80-90% of your month as the other 10% is for the week of your period and other times where you need to rest, have downtime or clearing/integration/deep meditation time.)

If they are operating at that monthly 80-90%, that means that all of these areas are in alignment, so congratulations!

Before we get started with the ceremony, here are some traits of your inner union (both your inner masculine and feminine aspects treating each other with, and you treating yourself and others with): unconditional love, integrity, gratitude, honor, respect, honesty, compassion, joy, happiness, service to the highest good, healthy expression, etc.

And now, let's get to the fun part - consciously activating our own Inner Union!

Section VI:

Inner Divine Union Meditation

Let's go meditate in your sacred healing garden with your inner feminine. Allow yourself to breathe in and out, feeling yourself being taken deep into your body, into your being.

Visualize yourself walking down that hallway towards the pulsating golden door and as you come to stand in front of the golden door with symbols and shapes on it, you turn the golden knob.

You step through back into your sacred healing space.

Has your sacred healing space changed? Is the energy clearer or more alive, perhaps more golden or shimmery? Are there more water or plants or trees? What do you notice?

Wonderful.

Now, bring forward your own inner feminine today. How is she doing? What's she look like? Is she happier and feeling more loved? More confident and relaxed? More flowing and inspired? Good. Now let her relax and step to one side.

Now bring forward your inner masculine. How is he doing? What's he look like? Is he happier and feeling more loved? More confident and relaxed? Feeling more structured and taking inspired actions?

Good.

Now have your inner masculine come towards your inner feminine. Notice how he lovingly looks and speaks to her. How does he touch her? How does she look at him and touch him?

If there is anything that comes up to be cleared here, allow it to happen. If he feels domineering or angry, what does he have to say? If she feels domineering or angry, what does she want to say? Then stop this meditation and go write more letters to each of them to get to the root of this.

However, if they react to each other with love and affection, adoration and respect - this is a wonderful sign!

That means you are ready to ask them to join together - to come into inner union. So ask them. "My inner feminine and inner masculine, I am ready for you to come into sacred union within me."

Your inner feminine will turn to your inner masculine and smile and say "I'm ready! What do you need from me to show up in support and take care of me?"

Witness his response to her.

Your inner masculine will turn to your inner feminine and smile and say "I'm ready! What do you need from me to feel my support and to let me take care of you?"

Witness her response to him.

As you see them join hands and embrace, with knowing and Divine Love, we will now call in all of your spirit team and guides, your highest self and light council, and everyone working with you who serves the light only.

We call them in across all time and space, to witness this act of inner union and unconditional love.

Section VI:

We call in your angels and Source to witness this commitment and dedication to the holiness of this Divine Union and to bless it with their presence, love and support.

As they all come in to support you, notice who comes in to stand directly behind your inner feminine and masculine during this ceremony. *This can include Mary Magdalene and Yeshua, or Isis and Osiris, Shekinah and Metatron, or going back even further to the beginning of Divine Union. There are no judgments here.*

These are your blueprints of Divine Feminine and Divine Masculine, your sacred Divine Union blueprint.

Ask the beings standing behind your inner feminine and masculine if there is anything else for you to do today in this moment of inner Divine Union, if there is anything else that needs to be seen, cleared or healed here for full activation into your inner union.

Wait for their response and follow their directions.

If there is nothing that needs to be done, it is time to complete the ceremony. Say out loud:

"I ask that this internal union is protected across all time and space by all who are gathered here today in this sacred space. I ask for the clarity to love and cherish each energy, and respect their words and feelings. I ask to be a beacon of love and light for those who need to witness the power of Divine Love and Divine Union within myself. And so it is. Thank you, thank you, thank you!"

Thank all of your guides, angels, Source, and team for showing up for you today.

Ask your highest self if there is anything you need to know after this ceremony.

And then notice if anything has changed in your healing garden. Has it changed into another space or has anything grown larger or evolved into something else?

Now see yourself walking towards the door and open the door. Walk through the doorway and close the door behind you. You can return here at any time. This is your space that is unique to your soul.

Walk down the hallway back towards where you came from. Then look down at your feet. See roots growing from your legs, your feet, your root chakra, down into Lady Gaia, into the core of the Great Mother.

Take a deep breath in and open your eyes.

For the next 5-10 minutes, journal everything that was said to you in that healing space, everything that you needed to do, and about the ceremony itself. Feel and receive new information as you do this.

Thought Exercise (version 2):

In 2 years, who are you, where do you live, what are you doing every day, what are you wearing, how much are you laughing, romance, etc.? (*Go into big detail here. Imagine it. See yourself. Feel yourself. See my hints below.*)

How has this changed from the first time you did it further up in this workbook?

Section VI:

- What are you wearing?
- How is your energy?
- Where is your home or homes?
- What's your dream home look like - big house? Stone streets? Next to mountains, trees or water? More than 1 home?
- How much are you outside? Is it sunny?
- What does it smell like where you live? What are the tastes? What do you hear?
- Who are you with?
- How do you feel with your Divine Counterpart? What are the emotions you have when you look at HIM/HER? What is their energy like?
- Do you have animals?
- Do you have a housekeeper, etc.
- What are you eating? Are you cooking?
- I am singing and dancing around the house.
- I am co-creating healing retreats with 2 aligned sisters.
- I am meditating and enjoying my energy work.
- I am...

Create a voice note from what you wrote down above - the "future you" scene - that you listen to daily before you get out of bed and before you sleep.

Section VII: FAQs and Next Steps

Section VII:

As you continue to disconnect even further from the 3D world and claim your 5D vibration, your state of BEing, you will continue to see people, places and things fall away from you. *We are advancing in the coming years and decades by continuing to ascend into 6D+ states of being.*

The more inner work you face, clear and integrate, the more you will align to your TRUTH.

You are here to fully express, Divine Feminine. You are here to embrace all of your gifts, your soul desires, your purpose, your words… all of it. There is nothing that you cannot achieve if it is fully aligned to your soul. You are the light in the darkness and you are walking this path in blind faith and the deep knowing that you are here to be in Divine Union.

The key is to remember that everything is energy. In order for something to manifest in the physical world, it must be *felt* energetically first. And felt consistently (not just one day here and there, or for a few minutes every now and then). If the feelings are not constant, the energetic vibration isn't constant, and therefore it cannot physically appear.

Below is a checklist for you to check off after you've completed the practices in this workbook *(you might be nudged by your higher self to come back to certain practices repeatedly until clearing or healing is completed for the time being. Inner Union is a state of consistent initiations, activations and clearings as we evolve throughout this lifetime, so layers are cleared as we are ready to let them go).*

Foundational CHECK LIST

- [ ] HEALED CHILDHOOD TRAUMA & WOUNDS
- [ ] DEVELOPED SELF-SOVEREIGNTY & SET HEALTHY BOUNDARIES
- [ ] HEALED INNER MASCULINE & FEMININE ASPECTS
- [ ] COMPLETED SHADOW WORK & INTEGRATED EGO
- [ ] ALIGNED WITH YOUR HIGHER SELF & CORE VALUES
- [ ] EMBRACED YOUR FEMININE WISDOM & POWER
- [ ] DEVELOPED INTUITION & LISTEN TO YOUR INNER GUIDANCE
- [ ] ACTIVATED YOUR SPIRITUAL GIFTS TO SERVE THE HIGHEST GOOD
- [ ] DEVELOPED SELF-CONFIDENCE, SELF-ACCEPTANCE, & SELF-LOVE
- [ ] ACHIEVED BALANCE & HARMONY WITHIN YOURSELF
- [ ] LET GO OF CONTROL & ATTACHMENTS TO OUTCOMES
- [ ] EXPERIENCED INNER UNION WITHIN

Section VII:

Remember to look at what is the reality of your current situation, and to know that it is an inside job. You get to decide to change your reality and take the steps to make that happen.

Below are some other practices for reality creation.

Feeling HIM

Feel your Counterpart next to you, holding you or cuddling you before you go to sleep, feel his tenderness and love, feel his protection and provision, feel how he makes you feel like the most beautiful, sacred, feminine woman in the world!

Speak to him, communicate, play, joke around, etc. – treat him as if he is actually there and feel it to be so.

This creates your reality – this consistent feeling that he is there with you NOW. (*This should be consistent for a minimum of 2-3 months.. your reality is based off of what you were doing 3 months ago.*)

*Replace the HIM with HER if you are attracting HER.

Gratitude

One of the quickest ways to consciously create or manifest is to be vibrating at the frequency of gratitude. Feeling truly grateful for everything that we already have starts the process of vibrating with gratitude. This vibration allows us to manifest in the present moment much easier and more fluidly.

This gratitude practice works best if you do it for a minimum of 30 days in a row. Once you have done this practice for 30 days, it becomes ingrained in your system and you will do it automatically - helping you hold the vibration of gratitude throughout the day.

Whenever you wake up feeling unhappy or if you complain about something during the day, immediately shift into listing what you are grateful for in your life.

These are the daily gratitude practices that can help you shift your reality very quickly. *Doing these in conjunction with 1 hour of recorded subliminals or affirmations will supercharge this as well.*

1. Before you open your eyes in the morning, **say out loud or in your head 3 things that you are grateful for**. Feel that gratitude vibrating in your heart and body.

    - i.e. your comfy bed, heat and hot water, your friendship, the healthy food you eat, etc.

2. Check in with yourself during the day and notice if you are feeling frustrated, upset, or entitled. **List 3 things from the past hour** that you are grateful for. Feel yourself vibrating with gratitude.

    - i.e. completing a task, clean water to drink, met up with a friend, repotted a plant, the freedom to live life on your own terms, etc.

3. Before you sleep, as you are already settled in bed and have turned the lights off, place your hand on your heart (or hold a crystal that you will use only for this practice), and **go over 3 magical things that happened for you today** that you are

grateful for. *If you prefer, you can write these 3 things down in a journal each night.* Going to sleep with these positive gratitude thoughts helps your subconscious bring more of that to you.

- i.e. I received a nice compliment today. A stranger paid for my coffee. I got a discount on my bill. A new client paid for my services, etc.

Statements

We can also assist our subconscious by stating out loud our desire.

Before you go to sleep each night, as you are drifting off, say out loud, "I go to sleep with my person/counterpart/king/husband/etc."

Upon waking, say, "I wake up with my person/counterpart/king/husband/etc."

FAQ's

Below are channeled posts (2021-2023) from my higher self and my spirit team who are all about Divine Union being fully integrated in all humans on this planet.

These are for your own knowing and understanding of inner and outer union, for it to sink into your soul and to ask questions to yourself in deep reflection.

Not everyone can handle Divine Union.

The level at which you must empty yourself out, to truly be in devotion to love, to the Divine - is a level that most humans are unwilling to reach.

It is comfortable to stay in your pain body, to be always right, to "know" everything, to have no relationship with the Divine. That is what your body/brain/ego is used to.

When you truly devote yourself to Divine Union, you are taken on a deepening journey - inside of yourself.

You will face all of your own shadows. You will sob alone on the floor for days. You will allow the old you to die.

Why?

Because you want to come to HIM/HER as your true soul. In tune with your own inner knowing and wisdom. With connection straight to source.

Not as a wounded inner child running rampant and living with extreme ups and downs. Not as a pissed off woman asking "where are all the good men" or an unconfident man wondering why he's always in the "friend zone".

There are times that we must truly acknowledge where we are at and how much inner work we've actually done (or avoided).

I know women who are super into all things galactic and cannot ground themselves on this planet. Their nervous systems are shot. They want to die and go back to "where they came from". Yet, they want their Divine Union. Not understanding that the grounding into this lifetime, this planet, this body, is what creates a happier, healthier you. Thus, opening the door for inner and outer union.

Section VII:

I know women who say they are okay alone. They would rather focus on their business and their friendships. They will never let a man be equal to them. This wounding of women first, men last creates an inner division and also repels a man who stands in his own self-sourced, sovereign power. Men are not less than and they have their own gifts. This superiority viewpoint widens the chasm between the sacred unification within and without.

I know women who are very aware that they have a lot more work to do. They want to come into union, know they are coded for it, but have a fear around it as well. So they put off the inner work, they say "it's all divine timing" and live in a state of pain body experiences because this is what they think they deserve, deep down. So the inner union cannot come about, let alone the sacred outer union.

And then there are women who fall into false matrices of "everything is love and light", feminine dominance/the masculine must atone for all crimes, spiritual superiority (narcissistic) complex, and other anti-reunification codes/teachings. They are very wounded, and are being used to spread anti-sacred union feelings and division so that Divine Union is not anchored onto this planet.

Because Divine Union is the most powerful creation energy.

When two humans, beings, creators meld their energy into sacred unification (connected to the Divine) - they cannot be separated or stopped.

They are the stories of legends. They are unshakable and determined to create for the highest good of all.

They are creating lasting positive change on this planet. The Divine Unions are building kingdoms based in love, respect, honor and integrity.

Truly acknowledging and understanding your wounds, and why you get "triggered" or your ego flares up -> this is where the work is.

Most of us have had soul fragmentation (in other lifetimes, on other planets, etc.) and have been kept from sacred union on this planet for so long, we have forgotten what it actually is and feels like.

What it looks like and how it flows, expands, and how it is life altering.

And not everyone can handle Divine Love and Divine Union.

Sometimes the pain body (ego) wins. Sometimes it's more important to divide rather than unify.

Not everyone is here for love and light; some are here to assist in the slavery of humans. Some are here looking like love but are actually a succubus/incubus (when you ask to see their true form in the higher realms).

Every human chooses their path because, free will.

So understand what your soul desires, what your heart longs for, what you came to do on this planet, and what you want to experience here.

Only you know this. It's in your soul, in your dna.

Because the beauty of Divine Union (inner and outer) is for all of us to experience. Yet it requires your dedication, persistence, honesty and faith.

So - are you willing to dedicate yourself to Divine Union?

Or do you want to be in this same spot next year?

The choice is, as always, yours.

Section VII:

A Divine Union 🖤

He will never leave, abandon or reject you - because you would never do any of those to your inner divine masculine or to god.

He will always love, protect and adore you - as your inner masculine does.

You will never worry about where he is or what he's doing - he is always in his integrity and advancing his kingdom, not wasting time or energy.

You will sink further into becoming who you came here to be - further into your powers, your mission(s), your light/energy. You will shine even brighter.

His faith and his integrity are the foundations of his kingdom. He will only continue advancing and building his business/empire. He knows that his Divine Feminine helps him advance even faster.

Because a Divine Union is not just another relationship.

It's not a power struggle. It's not a "I'm always right, they're always wrong" relationship.

It is a true, honest, loving, energy filled, sexual, magnetic dance.

He is your home as much as you are his home. And I'm not talking about the home you grew up in or some karmic relationship home.

I'm talking about your best friend, your laugh partner, your lover, your beacon in the dark, your magician, your Divine Counterpart.

He grounds you when you float too high, and squeezes your hand to let you know he's got you.

He is the ONE - in all senses of the word - and you both agreed to this Divine Union eons ago.

It brings tears to your eyes to feel that, to really know that, and to revel in the magnificence of it.

To expand with that deep inner knowing.

That both of you have decided on this journey together, now, this lifetime. Both of you continue your inner work and leveling up. Both of you keep fulfilling your missions.

One is not higher than the other. Simply two souls with specific missions (sometimes intertwined) that happened to choose these bodies and this lifetime to anchor in Divine Love and Divine Union on this planet.

Because now is the time.

When the unions are together, they are unstoppable. They are the true family unit. They are leading the way for others to witness.

To show that you can create the life you came here to live; that you can shine in all of your glory and use your powers; that you can have the Divine Love of your Divine Partner.

That you have unwavering faith in god source, and yourself, and what you are here to BE.

This is not a simple mission.

Section VII:

There are many false mates or karmic people that must be cleared. There are emotional patterns, codes and brains that must be de-programmed and reprogrammed. Shadow and ego work, integrations and more. There are people that will try to break your relationship, or sidetrack you, or "be your friend" to gain something.

And you will do this work because your union is one of your most important missions.

Understand that your Divine Union is unbreakable.

Nobody and no thing can stop what God has brought together.

The Divine Unions are needed now.

It's time to create and build together in your union.

Align.

Not every spiritual person is in a divine union (hieros gamos).

Many are being sidetracked by a false flame/mate in order to keep them from their power and purpose. It's a struggle; some form of physical illness afflicts one or both of the partners, and they pretend to be "ok" and "happy".

Or they go back and forth with a person -> breaking up and going back, breaking up and going back - which is chaos. This also distracts from true unconditional love (of self and others).

Sacred unions are not hard (hard work).

Each partner continues working on themselves and knows that this self work is integral to their relationship, as is following their mission.

They understand and are supportive of their partner's soul mission(s). They honor, love and respect their beloved, as well as themselves.

The couples that have come to be in physical hieros gamos on earth chose to be an energetic example of unconditional love in union.

Currently, there are not many of these unions online.

But everyone is being activated. Everyone has their missions.

Every soul deeply knows.

And that's why you must wake up.

Only you know ALL of your missions. Only you know if you are meant for hieros gamos/sacred union on earth right now.

Only you know who you truly are.

It's in your heart, in your soul, in your dna.

We are here for you. We love you. We see you.

Welcome to love. Welcome back to Source 🖤

Stop expecting perfection.

When I say Divine Unions come together and it is better if you have healed your inner feminine and masculine, I mean that.

Section VII:

It's one thing to heal these relationships (with your inner Divine Feminine and Masculine), and another to expect that you're finished. That that's all you have to do - and let's be honest, most people have not done that healing/inner Divine Union at all.

The truth is, your Divine counterpart will trigger you (to see/reveal deep areas that need to be healed or integrated) and activate you (to your highest self, to other gifts).

That does not mean you give up everything for their mission (codependency).

It means you are aware of your soul missions, your sovereignty and gifts, and have an amazing relationship with God source.

The Divine Union comes together to anchor in Divine Love on this planet, raising the vibration.

Yet you cannot raise the vibration if you don't know who you are or why you're here.

Most people are in soulmate relationships, trauma bonds and karmic relationships. This is not bad or good -> it's simply a part of the journey.

The Divine Unions are different. There is no doubt, no running, no second guessing, no codependency or narcissism, no feelings of guilt, shame, denial. (Because you don't do any of that to your inner self/your soul.)

There is a difference between knowing yourself and god source - and being in a relationship that's comforting, constant in and out feelings, thinking about "what could have been" or be, and denial of the kind of relationship you're in.

Divine Unions are two partners who are very much aware of their missions and why they are here. They continue to expand and grow. Both partners talk to god. They are unstoppable.

That doesn't mean there aren't tests (to make sure you truly want and can handle what you say you want).

That doesn't mean there aren't roadblocks thrown up (to test if you sink into low vibes or see it for what it is).

That doesn't mean every day is easy. This is spiritual warfare and we came here for it. We came to be the light in the darkness.

The Divine Unions feel like home - because they are a direct soul reflection, a true soul counterpart to your soul. There is a deep knowing and familiarity, a deep recognition and gratitude.

Every soul has their own journey. Every human has feelings and takes different actions than you.

There is no perfect way to do this, no perfect way to journey or perfect way to get into Divine Union.

There is only love. That is you, that is me, that is source.

Keep going on your journey. Keep expanding and integrating and receiving. Keep becoming everything you are that's been hidden for so long.

Because when you come into your outer/physical Divine Union, the truth is that you will both keep learning and healing. You will both continue having joy, laughter and freedom.

So remember who you are.

Section VII:

Remember what you came here to do. *For most of us, there are quite a few things :)*

The Divine Unions are coming online now (into alignment). This year is the strongest year for them we've ever seen or felt.

And that's freaking amazing and so needed for the collective

It is time for Divine Union.

You know, deep down, if that is one of your missions.

Divine Unions - Tests of Honor and Leadership

The sacred union mission is not always an easy one.

We feel that it should be easier - as true divine love feels joyous, free and light. But this planet is in the grips of dense programs and there are many programs to dismantle.

Thus, the opportunities arise that test your divine union (inner and/or outer).

You (and your divine partner) will be asked to show your dedication to the power of this divine love template.

You will be asked to surrender time and time again to the divine plan, to the highest good, to blind faith.

And this is not comfortable. This is sometimes jarring and painful, and goes against the human ego's needs and desires.

But what you allow persists.

So if you aren't diligent with discerning who and what is in your highest good, you will experience more of the same (lessons, emotions, etc.).

For example, if you have a friend of 20+ years, or an older sister, and every time you speak with them they are negative, they gossip and/or they try to pull you down (into their energy, into their drama, into proving yourself...) you are asked to let them go.

Your old programming of false loyalty will tell you to keep this 'misery loves company' relationship going, but your soul knows you need to make room for a more aligned friendship/kinship.

And the choice is always yours.

You can choose to be around people, objects and places that drain your energy and make you feel bad, make you grovel or are conditional in their love or kindness (they only will show love/acceptance when you tow the line to their way of thinking or being).

Or you can say, "That is enough of that. I choose what is for my highest good. I choose unconditional love. I choose to be surrounded by people, places and things that show respect, honor and compassion. I choose my soul and aligning with my soul mission above all else."

Surrendering people, places, things - it is not easy and many emotions can accompany that letting go.

We have been programmed from an early age that we must act a certain way. We must hold onto objects because great-grandma's uncle's wife made them. We must put up with the disrespect, jealousy, gossip and animosity of our family, friends, coworkers, townspeople, etc. -> because 'that's just the way it is'.

Well that's not the way it is.

Section VII:

But what you allow persists.

If you allow disrespect, dishonor, envy, etc., that is what you will receive.

If you hold firm to your boundaries - your self love, self respect and honoring your soul -> you surrender what is no longer serving your highest good.

Because you know that there is nothing that can stop your mission.

There is nothing that can create a wedge in your divine union; nothing that can drive you apart from your divine partner.

And you will do everything that is required. You will take the actions needed, no matter how painful for your ego or off-putting. Avoidance and denial are not the way.

Because you are a Divine Feminine and a Divine Masculine. You are creating the New Earth. You have the power and the divine love.

And only you can be a living example of the truth, love and respect that is a requirement of the New Earth.

Only you can lead the way.

For the highest good of yourself. For the highest good of humans. For the highest good of all.

I write this because I have done this, and I continue to do this.

I have evaluated every relationship, every object and the places I reside and visit.

I use my discernment and my intuition to let go of anything not in my highest good.

I don't let anyone into my energy that is not aligned. I learned this the hard way. I become physically ill if I am out of alignment on this.

I don't buy any material object that doesn't give me joy. I don't visit new places that I'm not drawn to.

"I let go of any person, place or thing that is not in alignment to my highest good. I detach any attachments and align to my highest self and my mission. And so it is."

I like to put it this way - consider your energy (your body/soul) or your divine union as a new born baby.

Who do you want around your new baby? Would you leave your new baby alone with that person for a week (to be indoctrinated with their beliefs)? Would you allow your new baby to eat what they eat, watch what they watch, live how they live, think like they think?

If the answer is no, then you have your answer.

Stop pretending you can be friends with everyone. Stop pretending every material object has good energy. Stop pretending the location you are in is serving your highest purpose.

Start asking your highest self direct, clear questions - and wait for the answer.

Then take action.

Because words are words.

Action is what is required right now.

Section VII:

Divine Union and Universal Laws

I've been asked to speak on this to clear up confusion of how Inner Divine Union operates.

People come to me and tell me they are in their inner union, yet their person/divine counterpart hasn't shown up yet. Usually they've been waiting for many, many months and years.

When the inner union has occurred, you will literally go through the biggest upgrade of your life. Every healthy masculine shows up in support of you and all unhealthy masculines never even come into your reality. (The same is true for the healthy feminines and repelling unhealthy feminines.) There are tests before this happens, just to confirm you are ready for this next level, as is the way when we can either repeat a cycle or we've passed the test/move to the next level.

And this internal upgrade keeps happening because you are clearing more internally, and allowing more of the hieros gamos template to expand throughout your bodies.

This, in turn, allows your counterpart to show up in your reality.

However, if the inner union is not online yet, it pushes away the Divine Masculine. This goes back to wounding and what's actually running through your system (versus operating at your original template or programming).

❦ ❦ ❦

We know that when inner union comes into being, the result is a physical outer union occurring. This is simply according to universal laws.

However, the person who comes into internal Divine Union can choose to not come into outer/physical union (because free will). That is the only reason a physical counterpart won't be in your reality if you are in true inner union - because you've decided on a different path.

The two main Universal Laws regarding this "as within, so without" construct are:

The Law of Correspondence and The Law of Attraction.

The Law of Correspondence states that our reality is a mirror of what's happening inside of us at the moment; therefore "As within so without. As above, so below".

The Law of Attraction states that when you truly believe that you deserve what you are focused on and you are vibrating at the level of that desire, energetically speaking, there is no other option than that desire to show up in your reality.

And this is where it helps to understand your true soul purpose/mission, your soul lineage, your ancestral line, your current operating system, and your organic soul blueprint.

Because the only reason that physical union hasn't happened comes from what is actually happening inside of us - in our subconscious and our programming.

✵ ✵ ✵

Coming into physical Divine Union doesn't take years and years, unless you have so much to clear in your bodies (energetic, multidimensional, physical, etc.), in what you allow internally and externally, and in your belief system. Inner child, ego and shadow integration are also very important. Higher self and soul purpose embodiment assists massively as well.

Because there are layers to this work. When you think you've healed a wound, it generally comes up later to go even deeper into another layer of healing and clearing. Which is how we deepen even further into our truth.

Section VII:

Many of us agreed to journey on the Divine Union path during this lifetime. This agreement was set up a long time ago.

Yet many of these beliefs around it taking years or decades or whatever else - those are false beliefs inserted into your programming, corrupting your true (original) program from operating. Those false programs are to keep unions from coming together physically due to the magnetic power of 2 being joined together to co-create with the Divine for the highest good.

This is an internal "job" first and foremost. The Inner Divine Union will activate every area of your life and you will not settle for anything less. You physically cannot settle for less (because you will become ill).

♕ ♕ ♕

The time is here on this planet for these Divine Unions. It has never been more accessible. Freedom to live in this way is NOW.

You know who you are.

Keep the faith. Keep doing the inner work. Reach out to receive help from whoever you are guided to work with on inner union, remembering that embodiment, honesty and integrity are key.

Because as within, so without.

You are creating the reality you are living in. That is your power. So co-create with the Divine for your own highest good.

And for the highest good of all.

Much love and many blessings to you on your journey.

I didn't get to where I am today by accident.

I didn't just magically fall into my Divine Union with Stephen.

I devoted myself to my inner divine union.

When I say devoted, I mean I went deeper into myself until I understood exactly who I was. What I was meant to do. The path became crystal clear.

I cried, I purged, I fasted - I was initiated.

And I do that over and over again.

Allowing old versions of myself and old beliefs to die. Allowing my expansion and heart opening wider and wider. Allowing my power to increase.

Purging, crying, dying.

Over and over and over again.

Why?

Because I am here for my Divine Union.

Inner and outer.

If you are on point with your inner work, HE appears.

If you are not, you're single.

Period.

You can blame Divine Timing, and magical unicorns, and you're not where you need to be, and blah blah blah.

Section VII:

But he shows up when you've done the inner work.

Because that's when he sees you too.

This is the test. The test of if you are truly devoted to having your inner and outer union.

Or not.

I didn't marry the man of my dreams (that I had specifically written every aspect of him 9 months before we even met) because I waited for someone to hand him to me.

Or because I was afraid of the inner work.

Or because I denied I needed help or assistance.

I am the creator of my life. I created (with god) my union partner, as he created me.

I took the actions that were required.

I left my old self behind and contained my energy. I focused solely on my inner union and my relationship with god.

I died many deaths and walked in blind faith.

In the inner knowing.

Many women and men in the spiritual community do not embody (they have not been initiated by the fire) the balance of a sacred inner union.

Therefore, this does not appear in their outer (physical) world.

You can keep dragging your feet or denying you're doing anything to repel your partner and coddling your ego and old patterns.

But your life is created by what you literally are. What you embody.

Your energy.

And this is what shows up in your life.

Energy doesn't lie.

Neither does Divine Union.

It is the most powerful creator energy on this planet.

And you either devote yourself to it, or you don't.

The Ego and Divine Union

The ego is a tricky one and loves to play games and twist our knowledge for its own survival.

It continues to grow and evolve to "win" the human life "game" as well.

Which is why it can be difficult to discern between your ego calling the shots and your highest self, despite how advanced you are or how many years you've been on the inner union path.

When we humble ourselves enough to ask for help in clearing something we know is blocking us, but we can't quite figure it out on our own, we are able to move forward quickly. To "quantum leap" or jump timelines.

Section VII:

Yet the ego can blind us to being able to ask for help, because it wants you to believe that "you can do it all by yourself" and that "you don't need anyone to help you". Or that "you're okay alone and single" and "you don't need anyone".

And this is true for you if you're in a wounded feminine state (instead of consistent/embodied Divine Feminine energy).

❥ ❥ ❥

The reality is that discernment is necessary, as well as honesty with yourself.

It does NOT take years and years to come into your inner and outer union.

If it has, it is because your ego (and/or your subconscious) is calling the shots. There is something you haven't cleared, seen or claimed, and it is keeping you on a certain level.

Because once your inner Divine Union is fully integrated and embodied, your person is magnetized to you.

That is how universal law works.

When you ARE an energetic match for your Divine Masculine internally, HE physically appears. [Just like becoming a match for supportive friends, money, a new house, a desired job, etc. to show up in your reality -> it's an inside, vibration job.]

No if, and, or buts.

No running or playing games. No back and forth or denying truth.

He verbally says, "You are mine and I am yours" and he moves mountains to ensure you are together. (You take the divine actions you are guided to take as well.)

Your Counterpart knows how blessed he is to finally be with you. He has known you were for him from the moment he laid eyes on you. He felt you and knows you at a soul level. He's tapped into his heart and soul.

He manifested you as you manifested him - which means he did his inner work to become an energetic match for you too. Co-creation 🖤

♡ ♡ ♡

This is the lifetime where there are no more ridiculous delays or lifelong unrequited loves.

This is the time of the Divine Unions on this planet in numbers that propel humanity's consciousness forward exponentially.

We aren't here to play around and pretend we want to be single or in polyamorous relationships or what have you.

We are here for our true union and it's time for you to end this game with your ego, integrate it fully, and clear whatever you need to clear to activate your Inner Union.

Because once that is activated, your entire life changes. Your entire being is lit up. You passionately create because you are in your soul mission work (as Divine Union is one of your missions on Earth at this time).

And HE arrives.

That is universal law.

As within (your vibration), so without (your physical reality).

But how long you wait, or whatever it is you're doing, is completely up to you (and your ego).

Section VII:

YOU create your own reality in co-creation with the Divine - and also with your subconscious, your ego, your shadows, and anything else that isn't on your highest timeline that hasn't been cleared.

So is 2025 your Divine Union year?

Because it's the year of ending the karmic loops and all the other soul lessons that have been on repeat so that 2026 is a year of new beginnings and realities.

And, as always, the choice of your reality is yours. The responsibility of your reality is yours.

What are you consciously and subconsciously choosing this year?

🩷 🩷 🩷

p.s. Common ego traps are: excuses, avoidance, procrastination, settling for less, saying "you have done all the inner work", staying busy, repeatedly dating unhealed/wounded men or men with "potential", constantly looking at the past or future, etc.

Many Warrior-King men are not found in the spiritual community. They are out living their purpose among humanity to assist its evolution. Many have thriving businesses and careers, and have been doing some form of inner work for years.

Reframe how you think "where are all the real men at?" and FEEL yourself an energetic match for him. Not above him - his equal 🩶

Spiritual psychosis is not inner divine union

I've been asked to relay this information as we go further into this new chapter of co-creation.

There are many who are in spiritual psychosis who are seen as leaders in the spiritual community, those who have shiny "new" insights regarding galactics, ancient wars, earthly and soul tribes, etc.

I personally have witnessed this in 3 men (with large followings) who are charming, charismatic, "down to earth", and here to help people.

Their patterns have been this:

- They "know" the divine plan and are in a leading position so people take their "channeled" information as the word of god (no questioning it!).

- Go from relationship to relationship (aka codependency), grooming the women, never being alone or clearing their energy from past relationships, and using the women as shields so that people can't see (energetically) the areas they haven't healed/done inner work - and the women/partners pay for this by their bodies/health suffering.

- Are expert manipulators and take codes/keys - especially in large group calls and from 1x1 clients. They feed information to clients and create false timelines with them - to fulfill their agenda.

- Use their clients and "friends" to enact "karmic justice" on others so that they themselves don't face karmic repercussions, yet the person who enacted it does.

- Believe they are Yeshua, Metatron, one of the Archangels, etc. (Online, I have met 5 Yeshuas so far and 2 Metatrons...as well as 4 Isises and 3 Mary Magdalenes).

- Have the ability to create hierarchy because their mission is "more important" than everyone else's and they will "save" the earth/humanity/universe with their physical Divine Union, and that their DU is the most important thing on this planet and must happen now.

Section VII:

- Encroach upon the freewill of others because they "can see the truth" and they tend to be correct about things (again, goes back to how many people they get to help them create false timelines/realities).

- This list continues but you get the point.

I've known women who do this as well, with similar tendencies/techniques.

Yet for karmic reasons, all of these "leaders" have many followers and new people come to them constantly, thus the "leaders" are being fed new energy and knowledge/codes. Which is all a part of the discernment initiation of each soul, and becoming truly self-sovereign (not depending on information outside of own inner knowing).

All of these people have claimed to be in their Divine Union at least 2 times since I've been aware of them (with 2 different partners) over the past 5 years, making a mockery of what Divine Union actually is.

Divine Union is a sacred path that begins within first - it is not about being in constant relationships, or refusing to be isolated in order to go into the depths of your own soul and clear yourself out. There are initiations that cannot be bypassed in order to walk in this holy way.

Divine Union is to marry the inner feminine and masculine of your own energy and come into a loving, intimate and communicative relationship with source -> so much so that it does not require you to "be" in a relationship with another outside of yourself (although physical/outer union can be a side effect of inner union if that is the soul's desire/agreement).

And there is no time limit on these true physical unions ("must be done today!" is ego/false self).

Spiritual psychosis is a very real thing, and it leads to infiltrations, hijackings, and themes of grandiosity because the chakras being blown wide open simultaneously can lead to the fragmentation of the human brain, as well as narcissism and manipulation. Added to layers upon layers of trauma over numerous lifetimes and you have the perfect storm.

We are getting better at spotting this and understanding what this means when a person comes towards us in this manner. And we do our best to be loving and to assist (if we are called to).

However, in our own integrity, we cannot allow this in our fields - the creation of false timelines to suit false narratives; the using of a woman/man as a shield in a relationship (where you see the health of that shield-partner's energy and body deteriorate); and the lack of accountability for their continued actions.

Divine Unions are joyful, loving and supportive; free and magical, and a powerful pillar to behold! They transmute dense energies, work through problems together (in equality, not one above/more advanced than the other), assist each other, and are here for the highest alignment and thriving.

However, Divine Unions are not everyone's journey in this lifetime; it literally depends upon the soul, not the ego.

We are here to co-create with the Divine and with our soul communities. All over this wonderful, magnificent Great Mother Earth, in resonance with our soul lands.

And to do this, we remain in our truth, our hearts and our integrity.

If something feels off in your body about a person, trust yourself. Trust your own inner knowing.

Section VII:

All is being revealed.

For the highest good of all.

Divine Unions 💎 and the physical manifestation of the Divine Counterpart 💎

We know that everything is energy. Every single action we take is an energetic agreement to something/somebody.

So when you are wondering "Why hasn't he/she appeared yet?" it is a direct reflection of what you're energetically agreeing to.

This means all of you as in: you, your shadow(s), your inner child, your multidimensional aspects, your past lives, etc. - what is every part agreeing to?

Most everyone reading this has done a certain amount of inner work and understands that the focus of all that inner work is for living in self-sovereignty and inner divine/sacred union with source.

Which then reflects as the outer/physical Divine Counterpart showing up in the physical reality.

There are a few common factors I see in clients of why the physical manifestation hasn't happened.

💎 Chaos and stored traumas - the nervous system isn't regulated which pushes inner balance/union away, resulting in constant internal and external ups and downs.

♦There's a living situation (roommates, family, previous partners, etc.) that is keeping energetic ties to a previous version of yourself which keeps that old cycle on repeat.

♦Settling - going on dates with people who are clearly not doing the work (or who don't believe in monogamy), or settling in other areas of your life to "keep the peace" to your self detriment, or to not be alone.

♦Allowing old karmic relationships or previous partners to have access to your energy (via texting, calls, emails…) and responding to them (verbally, physically or emotionally).

♦Not living in your truth - your joy and love of self, along with your purpose is a key piece of what draws your person to you. If you are unfulfilled, dissatisfied, bored, etc. with your life or any area in it, only you can discover what will fill your cup up because that's on you.

♦Waffling - knowing the highest timeline decision/step but still wavering and going back and forth between what to choose -> so staying on the old/lower timeline whilst being able to 'see' the higher timeline.

♦Residual energy - from past relationships, patterns and old beliefs - that takes time to clear.

♦Organic template is still not online and more foundational work is required (which can include past life/timeline clearings, implants/tech/parasite removals, soul fragment retrievals/cleanings, shadow/ego integrations, etc.).

Section VII:

Your Divine Counterpart will be loving and supportive of you living your highest aligned life, because that is the life they are living.

They are here as your equal, your lover, your best friend -> not your savior or rescuer or father/mother figure.

The Divine Masculine sees his Divine Feminine as a glowing, radiant reflection of his own inner feminine - intuitive, creative, nurturing, loving, beautiful...he adores her and is so grateful for her in his life.

The Divine Feminine sees her Divine Masculine as a powerful, loving reflection of her own inner masculine - protective, structured, driven, understanding...she loves him beyond words and is so grateful for him in her life.

However, if there is no communication or relationship with your own inner feminine or inner masculine, that is reflected in the outside world. If a shadow aspect secretly hates men/women, then that pushes the physical Counterpart away. Etc.

Which leads us back to the point of why the counterpart hasn't shown up in the physical reality yet.

There is always an energetic reason, especially if you have been waiting on this to happen for years now.

This is why this work is so nuanced and depends upon each soul blueprint (the current life, past lives, soul contracts, shadows, multidimensional aspects, earth lineages, and core wounding) and the dedication to this winding inner union path.

As with anything, the more you clear in your energy, the more the manifestations happen quickly.

Yes, Divine Counterparts are coming together due to the energetic alignment currently on this planet. Yes, inner work is still required. Yes, keep holding the faith because this is one of your soul missions.

And clear your vessel. Clear your blocks and old beliefs. Take the step you're asked to take, no matter how difficult.

Ask for assistance and support from your earthly soul tribe. The most gifted teachers/healers/guides I know have a close-knit group of trusted people they call upon for support and blind spots.

We are here to co-create in these true union partnerships, in our soul communities, with our soul tribes.

More inner unions are coming online now, and in the next few years we will see and feel an even bigger increase in true Divine Unions as more anchor in these integral pillars for our communities.

It is time

No drama in physical Divine Unions

I have spoken on this before and apparently it's time for it to come through again.

For the ladies: you are not his mother, savior/rescuer, coach/mentor, fixer or provider, or "bro" (relating so much to his masculinity that you become it to fit in/people please).

For the men: you are not her father, savior/rescuer, coach/mentor, fixer or "sis" (relating so much to her femininity that you become it to fit in/people please/not trigger her feminist rage).

Section VII:

The reality is that true unions are based in equal parts responsibility/accountability and divine love.

There is no drama.

Let me repeat that: there is zero drama created within the union.

Why?

Because chaos (drama) is created by unhealed wounds/trauma and shadows.

[Drama can show up like: chaos, (explosive) fights, passive aggression, manipulation or coercion, gaslighting, people pleasing to keep the peace, extreme highs and lows, health issues (the body warnings of repeated emotional distress), blaming outside influences (other people, beings, energies, solar flares, moon cycles) and not taking responsibility for actions/deeds, etc.]

However, in your own inner (internal) union, you are constantly clearing and integrating traumas and shadows, deeper and deeper, layer by layer. You know that the outer world is a reflection of your inner state. You take responsibility for this truth and do the work consistently, without blaming another or outside influences.

If there is drama, codependency, addiction, repeated drug abuse (yes, even with "medicinal, natural" medicine) - these are because you have attracted that. There is a part inside of you that has called that into your outer reality, into your relationship.

So your work is to find that part inside of you and clear/heal/integrate it. For the trauma cycle not to repeat nor to continue onto your children.

Because chaos/drama in a relationship is not true divine union. It is the basis of codependency, dysfunction and trauma bonded relationships -> the same cycle as what we witnessed in childhood.

This is why your own inner union is very important. But it cannot be passed off onto the partner to do your inner work for you. It is your responsibility.

🌸🌸🌸

True outer (physical) Divine Union is peace, strength, Divine Love, stability and integrity at all times. It does not waver or falter. It has no ego. It is a bubble of power that transmutes the extremely dense energies of this planet.

But if there is no solid foundation with the inner union of the individual - there is nothing to build upon. Only an uphill battle that is constantly sucking energy/life out of you because you gave your word or chose this relationship (usually in a state of fear/survival mode, denial or codependency). For you to help or "save" the other person.

This is a false template/program and it is being called to the light now. Revoke it: "I now no longer allow trauma bonded, dysfunction or codependent relationships in my life. I now only allow true two-sided, accountable, supportive and loving relationships into my reality. So it is. Thank you, thank you, thank you!"

Then it is up to you to uphold this new reality that your soul desires to create.

To no longer allow yourself to be dragged into drama/conflict/stress/trauma. To step away from those who bypass or refuse to do their own inner work. To keep your boundaries for the peace and love of your own self.

For your highest timeline and your own self-sovereignty.

🌸🌸🌸

Section VII:

The true union itself is not stressful. It is free, it is love, it is truth. It is peaceful, calm and mutually supportive.

That is not to say there won't be a difference of opinion, but any disagreements are met with open hearted dialogue and communication from both sides.

You are free to express your truth, your needs, your dreams and desires without fear of guilt/shame/lashing/gaslighting. You are both expressing as your true selves, and you both grow together and keep expanding.

You both deserve integrity, love, respect and honor. If you have to fight for any of that in your relationship, what is the truth of the situation you are in?

The other person is a reflection of you - so what part of you (that you didn't even realize existed, perhaps) is asking to be seen and healed/cleared/integrated?

It is up to you to be honest with yourself, to sit down in silence with your soul and ask what it truly desires. And then to take your god given power and create those desires.

You are magnificent. You are powerful. You are free.

You are an embodiment of the Divine, across all realities, lifetimes, space and time.

You are Divine Love and you can create your union.

Bring whatever needs to be seen to the light, clear it, and allow yourself to live in true inner and outer union.

Because this is the time of the True Unions.

And so it is.

Divine Union on earth does exist.

Your spiritual, emotional, physical and mental desires can be met.

Kings do walk this earth, doing battle. Going unrecognized or misunderstood. Fulfilling their missions and building legacies.

Queens are amongst us, living their truth despite the naysayers. Healing and softening, creating work from their souls and nurturing themselves and their closest people.

Ladies, as you heal the divine masculine wounds within you and learn to trust and respect HIM, you allow more love inside you and create more space for divine love to flow.

Gentlemen, as you heal your divine feminine wounding and learn to trust and protect HER, you allow your heart and body to connect, creating a deeper space for love and growth.

This intentional (inner Divine Union) work allows your true Divine Partner to show up in the physical realm, just as it strengthens your relationship with source and you come to know that you are always guided, loved and protected.

This inner Divine Union work will require you to be very honest with yourself, with your soul, with your own inner knowing.

Your physical Divine Union will be a mirror of you. The work you do, they do.

If you are ignoring or pretending that you've cleared your energy, you've removed the blocks, you've retrieved your soul fragments, you've cleared your trauma,

Section VII:

you've integrated your ego, etc. -> then you are showcasing a lack of devotion, integrity and discipline.

Because both will be needed to fulfill your soul missions on this planet, as well as live in a physical Divine Union in co-creation with your person and with god.

✧✧✧

The sanctity of your inner union will allow for no settling, no codependency, no games and no fear. No lies, no self-sabotage, no regrets.

But only if you're truly willing to surrender to this journey, to this inner work, to your Divine Union.

If you truly want a King or a Queen.

If you really want a sacred union anointed by god / hieros gamos.

If you're ready to live the glorious embodied life you came here to live - a life full of joy, love, gratitude and abundance.

Divine Union is your birthright. It's your calling. It's your responsibility.

Are you ready?

Next Steps

Because the next steps for you should also have fun in them, here are a few fun side studies to help you understand yourself more (*only do it if it resonates for you!*):

1. Gene Keys (https://genekeys.com/free-profile/)

2. Human Design (https://www.jovianarchive.com/Get_Your_Chart)

3. Free Sidereal birth chart - https://cafeastrology.com/free-natal-chart-report-sidereal-vedic.html

4. https://astrostyle.com/learn-astrology/north-south-nodes/

5. https://www.truity.com/test/enneagram-personality-test

You must know your exact birth time, date and location (so check your birth certificate) or the reading is not accurate.

Section VII:

Recommendations for Further Study

There are many false teachers and gurus currently being exposed. Everyone has their part to play in the Divine Plan, but it is our responsibility to discern who and what we learn from.

I don't have any other books, courses, teachers or retreats that I recommend because I have not worked with anyone else on Inner Divine Union besides Source, Mary Magdalene and Yeshua, my spirit team, and my highest self.

I highly suggest listening to my meditations and talks on Insight Timer to assist your inner union journey: https://insighttimer.com/acacialawson. Please see the dragon clearings there as well, for our dragon aspects are valuable pieces to this union puzzle.

It is up to each of us to discern what is on our highest timeline and that includes every post we read, the information we consume, and the guides we work with (energetic and physical).

If you feel that you would like to deepen your union journey with me, please feel free to reach out to me via my website or social media. I offer different packages depending on guidance from your higher self and Source, and the level of initiation required.

If you feel the need to work with someone, please take into account their physical embodiment:

- Are they in physical union with their person/counterpart (ask your gut this question) because embodiment requires that once the energetic state is reached internally and consistently, it is reflected physically,

- How is their physical health (are they glowing from the inside out and taking care of their vessel),

- Does your higher self say it is aligned for your highest timeline and that you should trust their guidance, and

- Do you feel their words in your body when you read a post or information from them or watch a video by them? Or does it fall flat or does your body react with a constrictive or shrinking feeling from them?

Every soul has a different path for Divine Union and who we work with truly depends upon our soul resonance and soul contracts for our highest growth and alignment.

Remember that this is a foundational workbook for inner union. If all of the sections in this book have been completed thoroughly, and the inner union activation was felt and integrated, then congratulations!! You are ready for your next Divine Union level (because as with anything, we continue learning and growing into new levels)!!

I honor your resilience and commitment to this Divine Union path. Thank you for being here.

I see you. I love you.

Keep going.

- Acacia

Section VII:

Acknowledgements

To Donna and Julie – thank you for all of your love and support. You always read my books and give me feedback and I am so grateful for both of you! Thank you for trusting me and letting me find trust in fellowship. Thank you for being who you are. You helped me find the sisterhood again.

To all of my other Rose lineage women. You know who you are. Thank you for walking this path with me.

To all of my soul clients - this work wouldn't be possible without you fulfilling your soul contract with me and stepping into your highest alignment. Thank you.

To all of you out there who know that you are here for inner and outer Divine Union. Thank you for being here. Keep the faith and keep going. You deserve it all.

About the Author

Acacia has been walking the road less traveled for over 7 years now. She didn't know that when she left her career and life behind in NYC, in search of her true self, that she would be led on a deeply spiritual initiation path. In fact, she had no idea what Divine Union even was until Source told her about it and its role on this planet.

Her channeling, books, posts and words come from her direct connection with Source, and her past lives have assisted in all of her books.

This book was created from her own inner journey to Divine Union embodiment and marriage to her Counterpart, along with messages she shares with her clients on their own journeys.

Acacia is currently working on her fifth book and assisting her husband with his global consciousness raising wearable tech device called The ONE®.

For more info, please go to coaching.byacacia.com, byacacia.com, https://insighttimer.com/acacialawson, or facebook.com/acacia.lawson.3.

www.ingramcontent.com/pod-product-compliance
Lightning Source LLC
Chambersburg PA
CBHW060113170426
43198CB00010B/882